A Dance Horizontal

Praise for *A Dance Horizontal*

A Dance Horizontal by Kenneth Lyon is a treasure chest of versatile, stimulating poetry. Ken's exceptional ability to titillate, challenge, and touch the hearts of everyone who loves words is the reason I recommend *A Dance Horizontal* as a pièce de résistance for one's library. It's Ken Lyon at his best, and what "a best" that is!

Sharon Wolfe
The Ohs and Aahs of Aging, Who Woulda' Thunk?

In this collection, educator Kenneth Lyon, PhD, masters many historic, poetic forms to craft his own delightful poems.

Florence Cassen Mayers
The Atlantic, Poetry, The Paris Review

Lyon is a poet of great intellect, rigorous research skills and fearless in his use of diverse poetic forms. "Have fun," says Lyon. "That's what poetry is all about." This book is an invitation to join him at his playground. He writes about the fullness of our lives. He cares about poetry, poets, and his readers. That's us. When I read his poems, I feel included.

Rick Kenney, Desert Poets

A Dance Horizontal

Poems

Kenneth Lyon

Introduction by Robert McDowell

Homestead Lighthouse Press

Grants Pass, Oregon

Library of Congress Cataloging-in-Publication Data Pending

Names: Kenneth Lyon, author.

Library of Congress Control Number: 2023941518

ISBN 978-1-950475-32-2

Homestead Lighthouse Press
1668 NE Foothill Boulevard
Unit A
Grants Pass, OR 97526
www.homesteadlighthousepress.com

Distributed by Homestead Lighthouse Press, Daedalus Distribution, Amazon.com, Barnes & Noble

Cover & Book Design: Ray Rhamey, Ashland, OR
Cover art by Gabrielle Lawder-Ruedin

Homestead Lighthouse Press gratefully acknowledges the generous support of its readers and patrons.

for Roberta

Introduction

Robert McDowell

"Words in conversation are like beans,
One breaks them off where they are ripe."

A Dance Horizontal by Ken Lyon surprises the poetry reader—old and new—in many ways. This first book of verse by a wise elder is neither polite nor conventional. The poems are genuinely inclusive, breaking all the rules while (Walt Whitman smiles) containing multitudes. Lyon's poems have purpose; they also have an edge and that edge is sharp.

Some readers of contemporary poetry will be startled by what they'll meet in this Lyonesque landscape where the terrain is super-stoked by gender identity, by who is cancelled and who is not, and by who should and shouldn't be. Beware! A notice for you may already be in the media and the mail. To quote Theodore Roethke, "You may be Dirty Dinky!"

Lyon has a broad reach. His poems can be funny, even risqué, yet serious subjects rise everywhere. A lifelong educator with Jewish Ukrainian roots, Lyon strips away rhetoric to assess the travesty of the current war:

"there comes a time
when you must kill
when democracy

is invaded by a mad man
and every value that you have
is attacked by armed Russian soldiers
who don't understand why they are fighting
yet destroy your homeland
and devastate your people"

At a time when many published poets seem unsure about what they have to say, even about who they are, Lyon's humble self-confidence and self-awareness are restorative. So many of his poems are simply beyond versifying, beyond speechmaking. They are the cold, clear expression of a point of view that will make sense to millions as long as they are thinking ably.

This is a poet who sees everything, *everything*, and apparently remembers it all, too. His poem about summer camp, "Monterey," brings back every detail of those shared, adventurous, terrifying days. He even manages to recall unusual details (and in the process gets to name a beloved American dance icon), such as seeing "Maria Tallchief dance at Jacob's Pillow." The summer camp experiences of many, myself included, were far less fortunate. Facebook, the kitchen, the madhouse, homelessness, hunger, UFOs, ghosts, old age...nothing is immune to imaginative observation and interpretation. Even Lyon's ekphrastic poems are direct and refreshing, lacking the guile and weighty rhetoric of many poets and academically trained observers.

There is utility to these poems ("CPAP," for instance). Not the most promising subject for a poem? With rhyme and wit, Lyon roars:

"Is this really a disease
Or just some made up apnea crapnea
What did the cavemen do

When they couldn't go to another room
Their wives hitting them with a wooden broom
To get them to shut up and start breathing again"

As one sees, Lyon's rhymes can be casual, yet another example of this poet bending 'the rules' to achieve enlivening effects. Lyon also thrives in another traditionally difficult kind of poem. Understated, accurate narratives like "The Florist" and "Bumps in the Road" accomplish what poems so often fail to do. They memorably evoke and remind us of important song-stories of life that are right in front of us.

There are impressive experiments such as "The Chihuly Museum" and "A Perfect Square." The poet even manages to rhyme 'fasciitis' with 'laryngitis.' Who wouldn't want to do that? There is a seven-sonnet sequence that examines aging and declining health, and an exquisite love poem, "Ylang-ylang," where wooing involves the purchase of a special perfume. There are many examples of how adept Lyon really is at keeping the line moving, such as this: "I walked downtown ate chow mein/With students smoking Marlboros/Speaking English laughing drinking beer." This is skillfully written yet calls the subtlest of attention to its making. There is even a nod to the Lone Ranger, and another that is dear to me, to Gail Davis, the TV actress who played Annie Oakley long, long ago.

Among other favorites, I must mention "After the Holocaust," "Meandering Jew," "My Jewish Ancestry by Nadab Ephraim Buba translated from Bantu," "Finally," "The Kiss of the Sixties," "Marijuana Melody," "When Parents Die," and "An Open Bed in Memory Care." Here is another, "Domiciled in the Madhouse," in its entirety:

"They walk their wolf every morning
And clean their wildcat's litter,

Their neighbors frown with disdain,
  Comment that they are bitter.
They built a fence around their yard
  And wire it with juice,
Postal workers keep away
  Afraid the pets will get loose.

They are the definition of miserable
  Have lost all their joyfulness,
A far cry from hospitable,
  The meals they cook are poisonous.
They sit in silence when they eat,
  Shovel food into their mouths,
All their thoughts are obsolete
  Every behavior uncouth.

How do we care for this couple,
  Show them things can improve,
When they are everything but supple,
  And constantly disapprove?
Do we just let them sit in squalor,
  Drift deeper into insanity,
Or do we hand them a dollar
  Thinking we've helped humanity?"

This poem, especially the beginning, makes me think of its kinship with a Tom Waits fever-dream. A poem, a potent vessel for compassion, curiosity, confusion, empathy, observes human reactions, their starts, stops, stumbles and recoveries with unusual tenderness. I think of a simple directive, so often lost these days—*Do the right thing.*

Lyon is always compassionately and avidly searching for what he calls "our common deformity." For example, the engaging child we first encounter in many of the poems in this collection's first section is isolated in an Us vs. Them reality. Dreamscapes are spooky; so is the world awake. The child experiencing all of it is often suspicious. At times, he comes across as almost a conspiracy theorist, worrying himself about adult plans for him and his tribe of pre-pubescents. Even years later, an adult himself, he must still "wake up early and check the covers/find out who is awake or asleep/and what they are planning to do to him..." This 21st century anxiety, born of the 20th century's relentless racism, war and genocide, is deep in this poet's core, yet the art of poetry establishes a process of rehabilitation that actually stands a chance at transforming evil to good. This is an altogether admirable intention for a contemporary poet.

Let me get to this book itself by mentioning one other poem. "Autobiography of a Poem" acts like a charm as it chronicles meeting and falling in love with poetry. "If I have a poem, at least I have a poem/And things are not that bad." Yes, that's the expansive, intimate discovery I seek in poetry. It's lovely.

"Eyes that looked into each other's eyes
Somehow knew that everything had changed"

from "A Dance Horizontal"

Contents

I

Future Archives and the
Resurrection of Extinct Thoughts

The Past Has Passed, or Has It?

Non, rien de rien, non, je ne regrette rien, … je me fous du passé!
Edith Piaff

Behold an amalgam of images,
a tapestry of blended threads
worn out by time
and faded from repetition,
a paradigm existing
        in retroactive visions.

Can you forget what cannot be changed,
and change what cannot be forgotten,
weave it into a different story,
a tale obscured by memory
trying to disappear
        and dissolve into oblivion.

The skeletons in the closet
shake hands with someone else's past,
haunted by what they can remember
and who they choose to forget,
who they choose to be or not to be,
        and what they tend to regret.

The past is worn like a shadow,
behind the scenes it lingers,
a worn-out colorless garment,
waiting for a time to visit.

        Pay attention to what it tells you,
        or you just might miss it.

The Best Poem Ever Written

Will turn you into an ocean
Underneath the sun and moon
Wrap you in a baby blanket
Or a white shroud
That tastes like forever
And somehow smells like childbirth

You will become a mountain
Climbing into clouds
That chant secret messages
Like the wind and rain
Songs that you have never heard
But know the melody and the lyrics

You become the sky
Surrounding everyone and everything
As clear as infinity
And even further
Reaching beyond the beyond
And touching what has never been touched
Unknown lands and thoughts
Daybreak and nightfall inside of you

Light and darkness
Lead you every step of the way
Life and breath, strife and death
All one in every thought
Written in every word that you say
Every day every night
And every poem ever written

Melting Pot

The Tower of Babel
has a gift shop in the basement
that sells Rosetta Stone in Farsi
Vietnamese and Hebrew
to weary travelers with pocket translators
trying to make their way
around the world
on a pilgrimage in Tibet
stranded in Tokyo
and speaking Gullah on plantations in Georgia
Sumerian in Mesopotamia
asking for directions in Mandarin
the time of day in Hindi
lodging in Guadalajara
Beaujolais Nouveau in Paris
sightseeing in Saudi Arabia
taking photos in Bangladesh

Tourists try to order dinners
in ancient restaurants that look like antiquity
and smell like the Spice Road
cinnamon ginger cloves and nutmeg
revert to pointing at an invisible menu
with illustrations of grilled meat

and rare vegetables growing organically
in a disappearing forest
fish that have never seen daylight
and wild game that once roamed the tundra
find their way into crowded taverns and diners
with street vendors trying to make a living

We babble to each other as best we can
playing charades for real money
gestures and contorted facial expressions
to let other people know that we are all here
on the same sphere
see the same sun and moon
chart our horoscopes in constellations
feel the wind and rain
feed our children
teach them to read and write
hieroglyphics phonics and phonetics to express themselves
Ay want yu tu understand mee
und tel mee ol ubawt yerself
speak to me through art and music
take care of parents and grandparents
wake up and go to bed
seek peace and happiness
avoid natural disasters
war hunger and poverty

Try your best to communicate with brothers and sisters
so that they can know how we feel
what we need and how we can help them
talk to us and stir the pot
with all the right ingredients
words thoughts and customs
ancient tongues that melt with flavor
simmer in the world's best recipes
and live forever sweet and savory

Glory to Ukraine

I put a blue and yellow flag decal
on the rear bumper of my Subaru
also one on the back of my golf cart
sent a donation to UNICEF for the children
there is little I can do
but feel helpless and angry

a great grandmother I never knew
raised her family in Kyiv
her husband from Odessa
my mother danced the Trotsky at family weddings
in America and baked chicken Kiev for dinner
I never knew what it was like
to be Ukrainian
until now with my Ukrainian blood boiling
I can't watch the children's hospitals
and maternity wards
reduced to rubble
damaged buildings evacuated
and millions of refugees

in my nightmares I get on a plane
a pacifist with a javelin missile
in my checked baggage
ask Zelenskyy where I should fight

there comes a time
when you must kill
when democracy
is invaded by a mad man
and every value that you have
is attacked by armed Russian soldiers
who don't understand why they are fighting
yet destroy your homeland
and devastate your people

where is the peace
that brings babies into the world
where people walk arm and arm
and return to decimated cities
to plant flowers and comfort the children

Running Away

I packed up and walked around the block
Put my prized possessions in a brown paper bag
That my father gave me for the journey
Pajamas and a change of clothes
Some underwear and a toothbrush
When I got to West End
No one seemed to miss me

But I was gone
Had had enough of rules
And things I had to do
Improve my penmanship
And go to bed on time
Get up and go to school
And deal with the litany of everything else
That seemed unfair and cruel
Now that I was more than seven

It was getting dark by the time I got to the next corner
I had to make a decision
Transform my escape into revision
And begrudgingly head west toward home
The taste of freedom
Dissipating from my daring sense of adventure

When I got to my apartment building
I walked across the lobbies
With little fanfare or excitement
A vacant parade with no one in the stands
My parents left the door open
But I still hid in the living room
Behind a plastic covered chair
Thinking that no one could see me
As they pretended that I wasn't really there

Sometimes total escape is the only option
Unable to come up with any other solution
Just pack your bags and buy a ticket to somewhere
Get a fresh start with your only baggage
What can't be weighed on a scale
But outweighs everything else
And a lifetime of too much detail

Monterey

I lived in a junior cabin
Not knowing the other campers,
At night we leapt from bed to bed
And swung from the iron rafters.
In the morning we had to make our bunks
With hospital corners to pass inspection,
We kept a daily BM chart,
Went to the clinic for every infection.

We woke every morning to reveille,
A bugle blaring on a phonograph,
Went to assembly to raise the flag,
All the campers and the staff.
Our counselors kept close eye on us,
Held us loosely in captivity,
We dutifully followed the daily routine,
That kept us busy with each activity.

Sometimes it was arts and crafts,
Sailing, waterskiing, or swimming laps,
Three squares in the dining room,
An evening campfire listening to taps.
Late at night, we snuck out of the cabin,
Tried to avoid the counselor patrol,

Raided Owaissa for panties and bras,
Strung them up their flagpole.

We shot .22s on the range, standing, kneeling, and prone
On mattresses, with a target in the sight,
Earned a junior NRA pro-marksman badge,
Practiced archery at bullseyes, breathing light.
Every Wednesday was field-trip day,
Three-to-a-seat campers singing on the bus,
A pre-pubescent song about drinking beer
While bouncing noisily over potholes and ruts.

> *A hundred bottles of beer on the wall,*
> *A hundred bottles of beer,*
> *If one of those bottles should happen to fall,*
> *Ninety-nine bottles of beer on the wall.*

Postcards to parents during silent time
Requested money for canteen,
Trips to Great Barrington, an Awful Awful at Friendly's,
Awful big, awful good, and awful deadly.
Swam every day in Lake Garfield,
Also went to the public beach,
Breast stroked a half mile to Elephant Rock,

After getting back, burned off a leech.
Earned a certificate for junior lifesaving,
Not able to pass advanced,
Almost drowned taking the test,
A near death circumstance in the Berkshires.

Other summer camps were on the lake,
Sometimes we had dances to socialize,
Hiked into town to buy candy,
Atomic Fireballs the tongue would paralyze.
Between the two camps was the Pine Grove,
An out-of-bounds woodland with mythical history.
The counselors converged there at night,
What they did, not too much of a mystery.

We paddled surfboards and canoes down Lost River,
Caught giant turtles and frogs,
Took a trip across the lake to camp overnight,
Feasted on s'mores and grilled hotdogs.
We hiked on parts of the Appalachian trail
And climbed rocks at Campbell Falls,
Short-sheeted beds and played fungo
On the big field chasing softballs.

Saw Maria Tallchief dance at Jacob's Pillow,
Walked planks at the fish hatchery above electric eels,
Caught sunfish, pike, and pickerel in the lake,
Ate spaghetti with meatballs at one-utensil meals.
Nametags were sewn in all our clothes
So as not to get lost on laundry day,

Everyone said saltpeter was in our food,
But we had no idea what that was anyway.

On parent visiting day, wearing camp uniforms,
Savored a picnic lunch with time to relax,
We walked away with hordes of candy,
Gourmet foods and exceptional snacks.
At meals we politely said, "Please pass the bug juice,"
And sang, "I'm a little prairie flower."
The one chosen had to climb to the rafters
As we hollered, "Growing wilder by the hour."

Last week of summer was Color War,
All campers placed on two co-ed teams,
Colors were different every year, like brown and gold,
With secret designated themes.
Both sides competed in sports all week,
Culminating in an event called Sing,
Campers wrote and practiced songs,
Supposedly the highlight of everything.

Puberty emerged modestly out of summer freedom,
Formative childhood had reached obsolescence.
An only child, I worked my way into brother-sister night,
And discovered the thrills of adolescence.
Becoming a teenager was a microcosm in itself,
An evening trip to Tanglewood also quite thrilling,
Where Joan Baez introduced a young friend of hers,
The first time I heard Bobby Dylan.

I now knew all the paths in the Pine Grove,
How to wind my way down to the lake,
I became a waiter in the girls' dining room,
A really fortuitous break.
I lived in a tent with three boys and a counselor,
We had a day off every Wednesday,
Made sandwiches for the campers at 6:00 AM,
Assembly line tuna fish and PB&J.

I started smoking Marlboros,
Behaved a little more arbitrary,
I could now go to the Counselor's Den,
Added swear words to my vocabulary.
I still heard the bugle calls,
Had a set of rules supposed to follow,
But now I wanted to lay my own path
Restrictions were too hard to swallow.

The head cook worked at the Waldorf in winter,
One night we stole a canoe, pretty shifty,
Paddled quietly across the moonlit lake to town,
Walked to the liquor store and bought some whiskey.
He made outrageous corned beef hash for the waiters,
And became a trustworthy friend.
Each day delivered another adventure,
Unaware that summer would end.

As beer bottles were counted as they fell from the wall,
I took advantage of each opportunity,
Riding the bus down the bumpy road,

Taking chances enjoying impunity.
The other campers seemed completely unaware
What every turn would be bringing,
They just followed the rules and looked straight ahead,
Would they get there before they stopped singing?

who am i and where am i going

what am i doing here
the small child asked
crouched in the hallway during a radar drill
putting his head between his knees
and not really wanting tomato soup for school lunch

waking up early on purpose every morning
before the clock radio turned on
lying in bed trying to figure out
who wrote the Bible and why did they do it
putting his hands between his legs
religiously in the dark

some much older girls came into the bedroom
dancing around from wall to wall
whispering quietly in their ghost breath
inviting him to join their dream
before the light switched them away

if he put the covers over his head
he would not have to face
the calendar that someone else wrote
to wake up and go to sleep
eat three meals a day
and prepare for an enemy attack

a century later he still has to be careful
wake up early and check the covers
find out who is awake or asleep
and what they are planning to do to him
what they write and what they serve
for breakfast and for redemption

Finding Still Life

At ten I was given a statue of David,
Shared him in fifth grade for show and tell,
Intrigued more about Goliath than Michelangelo
While David stood quietly in the nude
As everyone looked at his small plaster penis
And the pouch for his weapon slung over his shoulder.
I marveled that a sling shot could cause so much trouble,
And how small stones could take down a giant.
I put him in my desk when my presentation was over,
A retired Renaissance masterpiece in marble,
After hundreds of years going peacefully to bed
Until I closed the desk lid and accidentally broke off his head.

Dr. Chandler taught Audio Visual Enrichment
In the little theater every Wednesday.
We had to be quiet sitting in the dark,
Surreptitiously chewing gum, viewing slides,
And absorbing famous pieces of art.
Mondrian, Matisse, Modigliani,
Cézanne, Van Gogh, Gauguin, Monet,
We met them all once a week,
Venus de Milo and *The Thinker.*
Still I could not draw or do anything with clay,
Pastels, crayons, or watercolors,

I tried them all
But each one failed me.
I also could not dance,
Or sing or even carry a tune.

I cut my last class one day junior year,
Used a bus pass to get to the Met,
Viewed the Mona Lisa behind bulletproof glass,
Guards watching me for a few breathless moments.
She knew that I was only fifteen,
And I knew that I had to see her,
Her eyes had to see me,
Followed me as I walked past her,
Her mouth wanting to say something to me,
Her long brown hair and folded arms protected,
After more than four hundred years,
She was still in her early twenties,
Still sitting patiently for her portrait.

I stood in front of *Guernica* at the Museum of Modern Art,
And studied every person and animal in black and white,
Experiencing war and suffering
In silence, unable to comprehend
While feeling the brush stroke of violence,

The canvas of inhumanity and destruction.
In another hall loomed Jackson Pollack's *Number 5*,
And an hour or more in an abstract trance,
Transfigured into somewhere in my head,
Where thoughts were not imagined yet.
Paint had dripped onto a blank canvas,
That opened like a mouth as I leaned forward,
Wanting to touch me and swallow whatever it could.
Around the corner was Tchelitchew's *Hide and Seek*,
Children in oil playing in a tree,
More than surreal and deeper than I could see,
Come out, come out, wherever you are,
There was something in me that needed to be set free.

With his *The Persistence of Memory*,
Salvador Dali was speaking to me,
Showing me another way to look at life,
And not just life but my life,
Another way to go beyond what everyone else could see.
I also saw him walking out of a theater on Broadway
As I was riding by in the backseat of a taxi.
There he was in his moustache,
Illuminated by a row of spotlights.

I took a figure painting class at the Art Students League,
Six weeks with oils and naked female models,
Posing patiently undressed as still as they could be,
As I hid behind my easel in novice distress,
I did not know quite where to start,
And how to turn desire into art.

The written word became a stack of pages on my desk,
A still life if anyone tried to paint it,
Nothing moving, speaking, or breathing,
Without meaning for the time being.
I could pick it up and give it breath,
Pump its chest and try to feel its heart.
This is where my imagination starts,
And symbols sing and dance into your eyes,
Exciting feelings that you never knew you had,
Making meaning of emotions now unclad.

Antonym is the Antonym of Synonym

"We like to understand how electrons constitute a chemical bond between atoms."

Linus Pauling 1950

Cation and Anion were bonded
She very positive, the life of the party
Always smiling and upbeat
He very negative, the bane of existence
Always frowning and downbeat.
Their optimism and pessimism more ionic than iconic
How ironic that opposites attract.

They were like night and day
For or against one thing or another
Their prevalent relationship on and off
Up and down, in and out
Sometimes hot and sometimes cold
In a direction both forward and backward
Purely platonic, concrete yet abstract.

She was up front, he was out back
Trying to distinguish between right and wrong
Either the glass was all empty or the glass was all full
Nothing in between yes and no
Sometimes too fast and sometimes too slow
Yet not sardonic or demonic
Oscillating between fiction and fact.

They both read *War and Peace*
Liked ordering sweet and sour pork
Winning and losing no longer mattered
Either over the rainbow or under the weather
Their answers were always true and false
Every ending and beginning euphoric
Holding hands and making eye contact.
Cation expressed herself in simple terms
Pure and clear, energetic, and magnetic
Anion wallowed in complication
A manly messenger, amplified and valiant
They were single until they got married
Wife and husband, husband and wife
Had mirror image twins, Electra and Lyte.

The Hillocks of His

Wilhelm His (1831-1904) was the author of "Anatomie Menschlicher Embryo-nen," "Human Embryonic Anatomy," considered the first accurate and exhaustive study of the development of the human embryo.

Charles Darwin, in the opening pages of "The Descent of Man, and Selection in Relation to Sex," described a vestigial feature on the outer ear, originally depicted by British sculptor Thomas Woolner, as evidence indicating common ancestry among primates which have pointy ears.

Nestled atavistically on my Hillocks of His
Lies Darwin's tubercle unfettered,
A swelling of the posterior helix,
As if that really mattered.
Wilhelm His named my mounds,
Observed their growing dominance,
And then my deformity appeared
As a congenital prominence.

Wilhelm and Charles were interested in my hearing,
They exhaustively studied my pinna,
My outer ear with six small mounds,
Not bad for a beginner.
These boys were the oracles of auricles,
Investigating what was presumably apparent,

Discovering how to capture sound,
Without the slightest aural impairment.

Looking back to my embryonic days,
My outer ear was just forming,
I had a lot of things to do,
Like developing and performing.
As the hills fused together in unison,
One pair was slightly pointed,
Better that than other body parts
That could have grown disjointed.

My cousin has the same thing,
Something that we can endear,
She brought it to my attention,
Calling it our Spock ear.
It runs rampant in our family,
Her mother and grandmother, too,
We share common ancestry with primates,
Darwin was the one who knew.

So today whenever we meet,
Instead of shaking hands,
We touch our ears together,

We are our biggest fans,
Exuberantly celebrating our lineage,
And triumphantly appreciating our conformity,
Our outer ears and inner thoughts,
And especially our common deformity.

The Florist

The flower lady has a knowing eye.
She bundles lilies and carnations,
arranges rows of hydrangeas,
fragrant jasmine and begonias,
softens bouquets with baby's breath,
wipes away time with a feather duster,
celebrates blossoms and stems she has clustered.

Gentlemen feel an obligation,
surrounded by flowers, chocolates, and bottles of wine.
The chocolatier is stodgy,
the wine steward stuffy,
the flower lady is a valentine,
picking off the dried-up petals.

She never takes vacation,
never has a day off,
lives her unpretentious life in flowers,
vases, and potted plants.
She takes her apron off at home,
puts her feet up all alone,
and checks the calendar on her phone.

She has a look for every season,
special offers within reason,
dresses up for Halloween,
cornucopias for Thanksgiving,
Christmas cacti and poinsettias,
Red roses for New Year's Eve,
designing gifts that others need.

She makes sure there's something for everyone,
knowing things are not what they seem to be,
and that cut flowers can brighten the day,
can look fresh with just a little spray.
She knows that everybody has a story,
clandestine and hidden in disarray.

The flower lady puts on a smile,
always helps in picking flowers,
knowing that they will last a while,
to be presented in several hours.
Most of her customers barely realize
what she has done to brighten their lives
before she turns out the lights and rubs her eyes.

Bumps in the Road

A flagger stops traffic for the work crew.
She wears an orange vest and smokes a cigarette.
Her blonde hair contrasts with the asphalt
as if the sun came out at night
and burned a hole in the gridlock.
Some anxious drivers step out of their vehicles,
still running in neutral and parked,
looking down the line that seems to run forever,
wondering what the problem is this time
and what the flagger mumbles in her radio.
Is it a power line or a fallen tree across the road,
a work crew adding another lane,
a broken water pipe or a fatal accident,
a frightened animal that wandered out of the forest
into an unexpected flow of catastrophe?
The flagger signals what we need to do.
It is as simple as that, stop or slow,
it does not matter where we need to go,
or if it makes a difference which road we take,
which warning signs and barricades we encounter,
unless we try to avoid the traffic cones,
turn around and go back home.
Patience is not an option or an obligation,
as we imagine the brake lights turning off,

the flagger slowly spinning her signal
so that we can continue driving down this familiar road.
She will someday wave us on,
our caravan of weary vehicles,
flick the last ashes from her cigarette,
and solemnly tuck the butt into her safety vest.

The Freak Show

In the basement of Madison Square Garden,
painted turtles and chameleons
were sold as novelties.
Little kids watched the sword swallower
in hypnotized disbelief, amazed and oblivious.
The fire eater kept company
with ladies bearded, tattooed and fat,
and the world's smallest man stood tall,
a floor below the elephants and Bengal tigers,
the Flying Wallendas and Emmett Kelly,
absent a boisterous ring master
in a sea of pink cotton candy
and trampled peanut shells.

On the corner of Ninth Avenue,
two miles north of Madison Square,
and a block of bars from the newest Garden,
heroine was sold as a casualty,
as painted prostitutes swallowed fire
and staggered from man to man,
bearded, tattooed, and fat,
in desperate back alleys
marked with urine and semen
while some sinister ringmaster pocketed the money
in a trampled ocean drowning in itself.

The chameleons didn't change color,
and lasted about as long as the turtles.
The trapeze and tight rope artists fell to the ground,
as the hookers performed their tricks,
and the drug dealers sold their candy
to the children of former children,
in a dried-up circus that had lost its will,
where clowns were not as funny anymore.

Wishbone

Fishing in a chicken soup to remove a bone
within a skeleton that swims near carrots and celery,

bringing out the flavor of an ancient recipe,
and stabilizing the chest cavity for a flight

that is short, more like a hop,
like the length of a wish on a shooting star.

Maybe I should throw a coin into the soup,
unnatural like a simmering wishing well,

to replace the bone drying out on the table
that waits to be snapped in two

so that someone's dream can come true,
like steaming broth that wishes you were here.

She might have put a wishbone necklace on her wish list,
I wish she may, I wish she might,

one never knows what she wishes for tonight,
in her defense, if she tells, it will not come true.

She runs her wishbone offense like a football team,
a running game that is made of dreams.

The wishbone in my palm is not infallible,
its form both classical and flexible,

just as the chicken never dreamed of the butcher.
Would some archeologist in the future

behave in a way so intangible
as to make a wish by breaking my clavicle?

Cleaning the Chalkboard

The sound of fingernails scratching
Gives the warning that what's to come
Could look a little like what has come and already gone.
Attempt to erase whatever you possibly can
To eliminate the remnants of chalk dust
In your lungs that rasps like an old cough.
Use a damp cloth to wash the matte green,
Again and again keep wiping it clean,
Every time you write on the board what you think
Or try to draw pictures of the past.

Imagine a new plan every day,
Display it on the blank slate
Before you try to wipe it away,
Over and over but always minutely visible
Like a voiceless breath in air,
Heat that is dry,
Wind that doesn't move.

Be inspired by each fresh opportunity
To express your thoughts,
Written in ancient limestone,
White chalk made from decomposed plankton skeletons
That continue to be useful
And remind you where you have been
And where you need to go.

Keep it clean,
Always keep it clean,
Just in case you come up with an idea,
A fresh way to go about things
So that you can teach everyone else
That you have an inkling about what you are doing,
Where you are going,
And how you are going to get there.

Measuring Time

Watch the clock, set it for daylight saving,
scramble room to room
trying to be consistent.
Greenwich mean time
is really mean,
not even precise,
as each room is different,
on their own time,
and why bother
to know the minute
or even the weather.

I set my clock for noonish,
and I disabled the alarm,
no reason to be in a panic,
worried about being late,
remove the label "be on time,"
and cook something for so many minutes,
worrying about the altitude,
concerned about the attitude,
and how my eggs will turn out.

Time is draped in membranes,
like an egg suspended above the griddle,
identified by moments
that cannot be captured
or reinvented
or cooked to perfection,
in wishes that never happened
and dreams that were never dreamed
or set on a timer.

What a puzzle to worry about,
yet here we are ensconced in the past,
shopping for the future,
and measuring the present
with an ephemeral caliper
that hasn't even been invented.

Yin and Yang

Most days I suffer
From too much of one
And not enough of the other
Not really suffering
But mildly encumbered
Enough to make me aware
That something is off
Out of kilter

Maybe my *feng shui* is out of whack
Too much of this
Or too much of that
Oy vey my Ayurveda needs balance
My vatta is nada
My pitta is pitiful
And my kapha needs java.

Everything in moderation
Is more like cessation
Than sensation
I need a vacation
A new revelation
Look at things differently
Have an inspiration.

There's an app for Tai Chi
A mantra for yoga
Before I commit
Find the right outfit
Something to wear to the gym
Gyrate in the park
Flexible yet practical
Tractable not fanatical

Have some quinoa for breakfast
Mung beans for lunch
Drink goat's milk all day
Toxins expunge
Gluten free Vegan Keto organic
Where is the fun in feeling so manic

So today I'll be fasting
Not talking or sleeping
Avoid interactions
No promises keeping
My masculine will be feminine
For better or worse
Do everything I can
To not drive home in a hearse

Chaos Out of Order

My hairdryer exploded,
The toaster oven fizzled,
My DOC files could not be downloaded.
The toilet sprung a leak,
A smoke alarm went off,
My super glue was stuck,
The garage door opener wouldn't shut,
The septic tank was wasted,
A bolt had lost a nut.
The dishwasher went on meltdown,
The refrigerator on the fritz,
The garbage disposal had a breakdown,
The washing machine quit.

The gutters were all clogged,
The dimmer switch was fried,
The windows fogged,
The freezer liquefied.
The water heater stopped,
The pilot light was out,
Shower tiles had cracked grout.
The oven light shattered,
The furnace wouldn't heat,
Window seals no longer waterproof,
Ceramic dishes cracked,
Moss grew on the roof.

As one thing after another self-destructed,
I had to stop complaining,
No reason to get annoyed,
Just appreciate what I had remaining.
Things are things that can get fixed or not,
All these objects mean nothing,
Conspicuous consumption is disgusting.

They Don't Make Things the Way They Used To

I'm trying to find the they who make everything
Not in the Yellow Pages which they also don't make anymore
I want to call them and complain
But their phone which they don't have
Is automated and asks for my life history
Before I get connected to a human being
Who is really a robot

My voice is my password
And my annoyance is now intolerable
I push nine to hear the menu again
And zero to get an agent
But all agents are busy
With the high volume of calls
The wait time is more than sixty minutes
And the automaton asks for a number to call

Now my voice is being recorded for training purposes
And my cell phone is running out of battery
My nervous system is running out of patience
Like a drip line with no fluid
A bundle of nerves and cells
Exasperated by the way things have changed
And my inability to keep up
With perpetual built in obsolescence

And what really are things anyway
And does it matter if I collect them or not
Use them for what they are intended for
Or turn them into something else
Something that is actually helpful
Like a human being with compassion and empathy
A mellifluous voice that answers my questions
One way or the other

CPAP

I wonder what I could put in the humidifier
Other than distilled water
A Malibu Sunrise would be nice
Coconut rum grenadine and a little crushed ice
A diminutive tincture of Panama Red
Say my prayers before going to bed
My dreams however never boring
Wake me up more dramatically than my snoring

Which is much more sporadic as I lose some weight
Tangled in the hose that keeps me awake
When I toss and turn into slumber
That coils around my neck
Pumping air into my nasal pillow
That opens my airwaves
So that I don't gasp, snore, and bellow

Whoever came up with this contraption
Shooting pressurized air into nostrils like an oxygen enema
A crazy sleep-deprived scientist from the cinema
You won't believe what I invented
Cures everything under the moon
Hard to get excited when plugged into a machine
Trying to fall asleep while being tormented

Is this really a disease
Or just some made up apnea crapnea
What did the cavemen do
When they couldn't go to another room
Their wives hitting them with a wooden broom
To get them to shut up and start breathing again
Would do almost anything to appease their men

Still, I make my cocktail with distilled water
And crawl into bed with AutoStart on
Only a few seconds before I'm inflated
Floating off peacefully into the ozone
To hopefully wake up once more in the morning
Solve all the world's problems without even mourning

I'm Feeling Fairly Functional in Quarantine and Isolation

Placed an Instacart order,
Being shopped at the moment.
After it arrives
And I sanitize it,
It will be shower time,
And my wife will cut my hair.

I write more texts than ever,
Never know when to sleep.
The television comes on by itself
And tunes me in for a nap.
I must figure out what to eat,
What to cook or put in the freezer,
I'm starting to feel like a leftover,
Fresh at one time and now a day older until
The next day when the bread tastes stale.

For now, the clothes still seem the same
Until I do the laundry.
The colors slightly faded,
And my hands somewhat shriveled,

As I fold them into shape
So they can march into the closet
To stand at attention faithfully
And await their opportunity to dress up, someday.
Overall, my haircut came out pretty good,
Our marriage more refreshed.

Weekends have disappeared,
No calendars in the house.
Sometimes I roll over in bed,
Wake up and can only see the ceiling
Illuminated by an electric clock
Telling me whether or not to get up.
Rise and shine keeps repeating itself,
And I'm really ok with all of that,
The blah blah blah that resonates,
That has my blood flow from artery to artery,
My new haircut and plans for dinner.

The News Through the Eyes of My Facebook Friends

one sells liquid collagen and weight loss products
another pours scented soy candles
tells everyone when she's tired
others share their pedicures at the pool
various shades of blue green and purple
mammogram appointments Google Maps
directions to new restaurants
the fabulous meal their wonderful husband
made for dinner the love of their life
someone got a new tattoo another lost twelve pounds
in two weeks running every day and achieving personal bests
got married again gave a baby shower for her best friend
moving and selling their house before it was even listed
I see the same cat every week destroying toilet paper
the same cow the same baby getting older
growing hair and losing teeth craft projects from a shop
that sells yarn, thread, beads, and buttons
recipes with chocolate, sugar, and butter, deer in the back yard
who got vaccinated and whose children are back in school
who celebrates their siblings and who is outraged by the police
who is making music performing as a ventriloquist a balloon artist
building puppets and houses, a bowling team with new shirts
I have unfriended racists and political miscreants

religious fanatics and white supremacists,
so I only read half of the country,
but I see all the hurricanes and the tornadoes
the earthquakes and the volcanoes
the shootings and domestic violence
changes in the rules of the NFL, boycotts,
and executive orders, guidance from the CDC
friends and friends of friends who comment and reply
all blended together some have grandchildren
and others just disappear into cyberspace
"does anyone have any packing peanuts?"
a cousin tells me when she goes to Walmart
another how many miles she jogged
who went to the casino buffet for their anniversary
and had six desserts spectacular sunrises and sunsets
and clips from *Got Talent* around the world
poems appear from time-to-time and videos
that you have to "wait for it" and then the travel photo challenge
and your ten favorite books enough to drive one crazy
intoxicated by social media addiction
a mish mash of disconnected news feeds
that are important to everyone and identify who they are
and what they believe in, appearing every less than a minute
as a steady stream of what's happening around the world
and what you must know to be a part of it

The Clean Plate Club

Where are they now,
And how much do they weigh,
The members of the clean plate club,
Have they passed away,
Suffering from food disorders,
Prodded by their parents,
And responsible for the starving children in China.

Some of the members became picky eaters,
Forced to wash their hands and use a napkin,
Admonished not to push food with their fingers,
To mind their manners,
Not chew with their mouths open,
Eat their vegetables and save room for dessert.

While the club pondered the question
Whether to eat to live or live to eat,
World hunger strangled Africa
Like two giant hands around the neck
Of tiny children all skin and bones,
Their eyes telling a tragic story
With no answers.

That some have food and some do not
Is as wrong as ostentatious wealth,
The cruelest injustice on the earth,
From Appalachia to inner city,
As painful as a heart that doesn't beat,
A boy and a girl malnourished in the street
Begging with nothing on their plate to eat.

Foraging in the Frontal Cortex

A memory when you are young
like a nymph
in the unmowed backyard
can be revised when you grow older
and walk around in taller grass,
it may have a deeper meaning
but a loss of fertile freshness.

You might think that
if you were something other than who you are
digging in the dirt
and looking for knowledge
out of jagged stones and broken twigs,
the handful of thoughts
that you pull out of the ground
would have different memories.

Rub whatever you find on your face,
see how it feels and how it tastes,
does it remind you of something
that never happened
and would never happen to you,
something that you would
have to create
in order to make it real
and part of your life?

Dig deeper
until you find a hole within the hole,
that is where you need to be
and where you can finally
tell someone else
what you found
and what it means.

First but not Last

i.

Like a secret perfume, unknown and yet imagined,
    An untasted essence of heralded newness,
        The conception of excitement approaches at first blush,
            And with each new first a feeling of something fresh,
                Those first steps, that first impression,
                First and foremost, coming in first place
            For the first time, the first time for everything,
                Unable to be repeated or replaced.

ii.

First kisses, first marriages, and first children
    Take their places in quick succession.
        Who should tell their story first,
    And who should decline to say the first word.
        Their first day of school, their first job,
            The first time they saw each other's face,
                Their first love, their first lover
            Coming out of a shadow into the light,
    Losing their virginity in the middle of the night.

iii.

Foods from other worlds,
    From other people eating and drinking,
    Served with pride and nostalgia
        At restaurants where some patrons were tempted
        To try something new, that very first bite,
    First come first served, while others would order
        The same thing over and over again,
    Afraid to take a chance with something different,
        To upset a stomach, ignite heartburn.
    The regular every day was comfort food,
            Everything identical to the last time,
    Familiar repetition on a plate day in and day out.

iv.

Everyone's first was different from everyone else's,
        Even when their first time was together,
        Even if their first car was the same car,
    They looked at it differently, drove it differently,
Had different insurance and items in the glovebox,
    A scratch on the fender, a windshield cracked.
        Some were looking forward to their first first,
    While others were disappointed that their first
        Was not all what it was imagined to be.
Did that really happen, is that what it was supposed to be,
    Or was that actually something else disguised,
An imposter stepping in and proclaiming to be the very first.

v.

At first emerges a quick judgment and a decision,
    Was that so good that I would do it again.
    I'll never make that same mistake twice
   Until it happens and I do, maybe wait a while,
      Give it some time, grow up a little,
Think it over, move more slowly, resist temptation.
    What goes around comes around at first glance,
        And here it comes again, looking like a new first
And feeling essentially secret and aromatic,
    While the music plays softly for the first dance,
     You will be offered a second chance.

Not Every Monday is Melancholy

I drank a glass of testosterone
With my breakfast
It tasted like high school
No need to eat the eggs
As I was ready to face the day

The first girl I met
Was wearing falsies
She blushed just a little
As I adjusted
The front of my pants

The second girl
Had fake eyelashes
She blinked like an aileron
Ready to take off
All of her clothes

I was off to a good start
Undaunted energy
That could not be discouraged
By everyone else's problems
And the fate of humanity

Walking down the street erect
I was able to smile
Not step in manholes
Get hit by cars
Or even sunburn

It can be this way
No one wants to read about it
But it can happen
Won't be on the front page
But in a lively verse of five-line stanzas

Fortune Cookies

I eat lo mein once a year
On New Year's Eve,
Inaugurates my annual noodle portion,
The time to also read my fortune.

I do it at my own volition
Use it for my New Year's resolution
That I will be happy and prosperous,
Influence others and pay my taxes.

I am told that tonight is, "The best night of my life.
And tomorrow will be even better."
A butterfly wafer in the palm of my hand
Opens its wings to reveal
Lucky lottery numbers
And a small strip of paper with the aphorism,
"You learn from your mistakes,
You will learn a lot today."

I remember that Confucius said,
"Roads were made for journeys, not destinations."
My long and arduous dinner a delicious adventure
Complimented by printed revelations,
"Into duck sauce eggroll dip,
Give to waiter generous tip."

I finished the last mouthful, put my chopsticks away,
Read the next prophecy for what it's worth,
Always willing to play life's game,
"Be careful who you trust, salt and sugar look the same."

I sometimes ask for another cookie, a handful,
Need to be prepared for the following years,
As many as my fortune will allow,
Ups and downs, pleasure and pain,
"If you want the rainbow you gotta put up with the rain."
The first day of the year provides an introduction,
"The road to success is always under construction."

Once I got an empty cookie with no fortune in it,
Time stood still for just a minute.
I paused until I had to admit,
"The most effective way to do it is to do it."
So I took that advice, to "Go with your gut,"
Kept opening cookies no matter what,
Reading paper truisms and sincerely trying,
To "Get busy living or get busy dying."

Angel Food Cake and Devil's Food Cake

Someone shouted, "Food fight!"
And everyone ducked under cafeteria tables
As apples and containers of milk
Soared through the air like meteorites
Guided by Tomahawk cruise missile technology,
The particle board barriers and benches
Providing shelter from incoming
Pudding cups and pizza crusts.

As pieces of cake sailed toward their targets,
The fearful on the ground
Only had a few desperate seconds
To determine if this were heaven or hell,
The coming of the Messiah
With egg whites beaten to soft peaks,
Or a one-way lunch ticket to purgatory,
Dark and bittersweet.

Their lives flashed before their eyes, classes they cut,
Lies they told, and candy they stole,
Boyfriends and girlfriends, jealousies and travesties,
Shared secrets and clandestine meetings,
Dates on the calendar they wished they could do over,
Tears that came and went with every emotion,
And fears that resurfaced from this turbulent commotion.

Someone blew a whistle, and everything was frozen,
Even the projectiles were held captive in the air
Like a mural of a war that wasn't moving,
A freeze frame image silent as a snapshot,
A reflection and recollection that life has its moments,
And this was surely one of them,
One to remember, also forget.

Soliloquy by Father Time's Son

Don't tell anyone, do not share,
But something isn't quite right,
The way it used to be.
Something hides behind the door
Like dirty laundry, soiled and stained,
Unable to come back to life
And put on a fake smile.

Oh yes, I talk to myself
When no one's listening,
But that doesn't help,
Only echoes in the hallway
And bounces back
Like a shallow ripple in the air.

I need to snap out of it,
Man up, walk it out,
Pull up my bootstraps
Until they reach my stiff upper lip,
Grow a new pair and suck it up.

No complaints from me, not one.
I'm just fine, maybe, maybe not,
Trying to rationalize my way out,
But something's off,
Just a little, just enough.
I'm getting old,
Losing stability, breathing heavily,
Not aging gracefully
Like fine wine or cheese.

More like an open wound,
An injury bandaged
By my baggy clothing,
A tattered sweater
As I wipe my mouth on the cuff
And tell myself
That I am just an old timer,
Measuring what time I can measure
And breathing each breath
As it best suits me
Until the air starts to smell like death
And Hamlet's answer is, "not to be."

Speak to Me in a Foreign Language

People keep talking to me in tones
that sound as quotidian as an old piece of music
with more than half the notes missing.
I try to understand what they are saying, nodding my head
perfunctorily with common facial expressions,
derived from past experiences and practiced
with repeated imprecision, lacking appropriate accent
and emphasis begging to be misinterpreted
and twisted into a bundle of barely audible breath.
How I understand them is how they understand me,
ultimately symbolic and distantly faint,
as a wavelength fading in and out,
a radio frequency that does not tune,
a phone out of range that crackles.
When I get up to drink some juice in the middle of the night,
I pour it into a champagne glass
surrounded by a chorus of international dreams talking to me
in words that have no meaning,
and yet I know exactly what they are saying
and why they choose to talk to me.
No need to make a reservation as
I am open to the conversation.

Masks Cover More Than the Face

The fabric stores are slammed,
Fast food take-out has taken off,
Instacart is off the charts,
Everyone trying not to spread a cough.
The liquor stores are flooded,
Board games and puzzles selling well,
The irony is that some are thriving
While the rest of the economy is going to hell.

Some businesses are booming,
A nascent symptom of COVID-19,
Masks makers and telehealth,
Every possible item for personal hygiene.
Supermarkets are packed now that restaurants closed,
Clean air with little traffic in the streets.
People who have lost interest in cooking
Rely on Door Dash, Grub Hub, and Uber Eats.

Coffee bean subscription services are percolating,
Online tutoring has replaced the classroom,
Everyone is desperately searching on Netflix
Or video conferencing routinely with Zoom.
People are buying more treadmills and bikes,
Looking for normalcy with their lives to carry on,
So, they sanitize, wash their hands, social distance,
And become shopaholics on Amazon.

The kids are going crazy,
Not reticent to share their pains.
The whole family runs out of things to do
And resorts to video games.
The pets get their food delivered,
They still have their expected routine
As everyone else hopes for the best
If only there were a vaccine.

There are the lucky ones, healthy and wealthy,
Finding ways to survive in this time of crisis,
Hopefully trying to help the thousands of other families
Of those who have sadly succumbed to the virus.
The best of humanity tries to pull together
As people go about their daily tasks,
Assuming responsibility, thinking about others,
Social distancing and safely wearing masks.

Unable to Talk with My Neighbors

At my age some things are impossible,
climbing Huayna Picchu again,
leaning over the edge for a photo
of the Inca citadel or
trying to kayak in an inflatable rubber ducky
through Boulder Drop,
a class 4 on the Skykomish,
keeping my feet up as told
not to get caught under water
in the rocks.

My opinions have gotten crusty,
a callus on the lenient part
of my brain that can't tolerate
that kind of ignorant racism,
that can't accept oblivion
from those nice, well-dressed people,
affluent in their own desired world,
but well removed from
the reality of the food line,
unemployment, eviction, and immigration.

Leviticus is just not working for me,
unable to tolerate
this new generation of an old generation
who think that poor people can buy a house,
that the minimum wage
is sufficient for a family of four
or more, that illegal aliens are criminals
on drugs, married to the same sex.

I have no argument that will sink into their skulls,
get them to change their obfuscated thinking,
put them on a mountain top
or flowing with a rapid,
can they possibly love themselves
and not know what they are saying?
Callous disregard of suffering
with meaningless arguments that at a minimum
I cannot even try to talk with them.

Déjà Vu

The hero and the heroine do not live in a fairy tale,
No shining armor or golden locks,
Only stark and dreary,
Dull, dark, and dingy,
Skin more coarse than silky.

The hero has asthma and cannot breathe.
He limps around the house completely lost,
Cannot remember what room he's in,
Or what he came there for,
His hair unkempt, disheveled, what a boor.

The heroine has crooked teeth and drools.
She hunches over her plate of braised beef stew,
Left her glasses somewhere thereabouts,
Her prescriptions need to be refilled,
Cannot remember the last time she was thrilled.

All their families long ago died.
They have no friends they can call for help,
Their days are numbered on one hand.
This is the moment that they dreaded,
Not barely a memory now they are dead.

Should they both come back to life again,
Move around without disdain,
A chance to make the same mistakes,
They would not have it any other way
Than live life together in constant disarray.

Domiciled in the Mad House

They walk their wolf every morning
>And clean their wildcat's litter,
Their neighbors frown with disdain,
>Comment that they are bitter.
They built a fence around their yard
>And wire it with juice,
Postal workers keep away
>Afraid the pets will get loose.

They are the definition of miserable
>Have lost all their joyfulness,
A far cry from hospitable,
>The meals they cook are poisonous.
They sit in silence when they eat,
>Shovel food into their mouths,
All their thoughts are obsolete
>Every behavior uncouth.

How do we care for this couple,
>Show them things can improve,
When they are everything but supple,
>And constantly disapprove?
Do we just let them sit in squalor,
>Drift deeper into insanity,
Or do we hand them a dollar
>Thinking we've helped humanity?

Hotter Than Hell

The earth is on fire
Call someone for help
Provide every address on the planet
And listen for the sirens.

Around the corner comes the hook and ladder
Followed by a priest, a rabbi, and a minister
The last rites are wrong
And the bartender is out to lunch.

No one is tending to the icebergs
The rain forest is no longer reigning
As all the animals head for the ark
And the billionaires go to Mars.

The same people are in the restaurants
The air conditioners are all broken
How can they afford to eat there every night
And laugh with their mouths full of nonsense.

Whoever believes ignorance is bliss
Has never touched a hot stove
The stomach of the earth in hunger
Or burned themselves praying for others.

Regulate the thermostat before it's too late
Pay the massive heating bill in arrears
Wake up to the alarm clock of natural disasters
No time to be passive, no time to sit and wait.

After the Holocaust

On the upper west side of Manhattan,
   all of my Jewish friends celebrated Christmas.
We had a live tree in our living room,
   bought at a stand on Broadway in the snow.
My mother strung popcorn and cranberries
   for decoration after putting away our extra Chanukah candles.
I had no idea then why my father
   would not buy anything made in Germany or Japan.
He had taken some black and white photographs
   in Hiroshima during the war,
   kept them in a jewelry box on top of his dresser
   along with dog tags and a bullet
   that he looked at every morning.

His father, born in Germany on Christmas Day,
   landed in America at Ellis Island.
We celebrated his birthday every year
   with cold cuts at his apartment.
In the morning I would call my best friend
   to compare what we got for presents.
His father had shortened their last name
   to not be identified as Jewish
   like so many others.
I would walk down Fifth Avenue
   and look at the window displays,

everything lit up and alive,
    all the stores playing "Silent Night."
Another friend's mother who lived across the street
    had numbers tattooed on her forearm,
    a mystery to me at the time.

In elementary school I discovered a book
    in the library about Auschwitz,
    Dachau, and other camps,
    the word "Hell" in the title.
I read how the Nazis tortured men,
    women and children brought to gas chambers
    in cattle cars.
I kept coming back to take that book
    from the shelf and read a few pages
    of hatred, fear, and darkness.

At Sunday School, I was elected President of Temple City,
    I couldn't sing but was put in the junior choir anyway.
Jewish delis smelled like home,
    as I got lectured regularly to grow up and marry a nice Jewish girl.
Teddy, my Bar Mitzvah buddy,
    was blown up in the East Village as a Weatherman.
Years later a drunk in my college dorm called me a Jew bastard.

Religion was more than a temple, observing the Sabbath,
    memorizing the Ten Commandments,
    thou shalt not and thou shalt not.
I could sort of read Hebrew, not knowing what it meant,
    figure out the vowels, chant memorized prayers,
    order Jewish food and date girls who weren't Jewish.
Persecution had developed as an institution,
    and I belonged to those chosen people
    who for some reason incurred anger and wrath
    as part of their history.

Looking back I could not look back
    far enough or really get it,
    could not place myself in the history
    of what was wrong with the world
    and what was wrong with people.
I stopped going to temple,
    still celebrated the holidays,
    could recite the ten commandments by rote,
    cook traditional meals,
    salvage remnants of my cultural heritage,
    and cope with anti-Semitism.

My second wife became a Jew by choice,
   converted and married a nice Jewish boy,
   did not inherit prejudice by birth,
   though slandered by some other Jews as a convert.
Every night she puts on her *schmata*,
   and often I use some Yiddish expressions,
   tsuris is something that any Jew can understand,
   like inside the walls of Holocaust museums,
   the relevance of remembrance
   of the millions murdered who practiced their faith
   and did not deserve their destiny.

Meandering Jew

We made love to our souls in bed,
and as she moaned into the mattress,
grasping ivory percale sheets,
I checked the box married white male.

The IRS envisions me fornicating jointly,
not a dual status alien,
not reveling in other data bases,
not American Indian or Alaska Native,
Asian Black or African American,
Hispanic or Latino,
Native Hawaiian or Other Pacific Islander,
just straight not gay bisexual or transgender,
no alcohol or drug use anymore,
simply Caucasian from Eastern Europe
presenting as white
unless I've been in the sun or forgot to shave.

I can relate to those other sexy boxes,
can hear their love stories and feel their pain,
their moments of joy discovering who they are,
while I walk down the street without hate,
and no one knows who I am,
unidentifiable like an anonymous pronoun,
my accent indistinguishable
unless I talk fast and need to get things done in a hurry.

Spread your arms and legs,
open your mind to the sound of humanity,
and take what comfort
this old white Jewish man can give,
one who has eaten manna from heaven,
a Sagittarian septuagenarian,
one who checked the box Jewish circumcised bar mitzvahed.

My Jewish Ancestry
by Nadab Ephraim Buba
translated from Bantu

"Karibu, hujambo," I am pleased to welcome you,
My name is from Judea,
"Nakutakia siku njema!"
I wish that your day be a nice one,
And I welcome you to my history
And my one holy day a week.
The cohanim brought me to South Africa
From Senna to read the Torah
A long, long time ago
With the members of my clan.

I fish Lake Victoria,
Grill tilapia for dinner to give me strength.
The power of the crocodile is in the water,
But the power of man is in the mind.
I plant the croplands and roam the rainforest,
Feast on banana, taro, and yam,
I avoid eating pork and other piglike animals,
Especially the hippopotamus.

We practice circumcision
And fight for our human rights,
Protect indigenous peoples
And live with many conflicts.
Words in conversation are like beans,
One breaks them off where they are ripe.

My ancestors taught me to see daylight,
Follow the commandments and live
With our many burdens and hard times from the past,
As one who suffers from diarrhea, is not afraid of the dark,
And we welcome every day as a new one.

My family is blessed and prosperous,
My wife speaks to me kindly every new day,
I have learned that a woman's clothes
Are the price her husband pays for peace,
And I always say to her, "Ninakupenda,"
I love you, for one language is never enough.

Yahrzeit

Candles talk for twenty-four hours
Remind you that you can do anything
That you put your mind to
When you walk by in the middle of the night
And in the early morning

They have a way
Of bringing the past to life
Flickering visions of mothers and fathers
Aware that we have become our parents
With all their idiosyncrasies
Habits and words of advice

You can see their faces
And hear their voices
Putting you to sleep
Waking you up
Like a séance
Chanting in solitude for a day

And then they're gone
For another year
And you're on your own
Trying to make sense
Of all your gestures and expressions
Attributes and deficits

I bought you a candle
Light it with a match
A year after I'm gone
Take out the book
Read the prayer
And sometime in the next year
Buy another one.

Speeding Citations

Got pulled over recently
For reckless writing,
Under the influence indecently,
Not arrested,
Talked myself out of it,
No fine,
My poetic license,
Not suspended,
I just needed a break.

A crumpled get-out-of-jail card
Still in the glovebox,
Plates renewed for another year,
Battery charged, wipers replaced,
All fluids topped off,
Brakes got new pads, tires rotated,
Fresh ink in my pen,
A pad of paper in my pocket.

I'm back on the road,
Pedal to the metal,
Without rhyme or reason,
It's Grand Prix season,
In the outside lane lapping the field,
With new ideas inside my brain,
And shifting gears in furious rain.

Do you ever know where you're going
When you start driving,
What you're writing about
When you start writing,
Navigating for the next line,
GPS for the rhythm and rhyme,
Getting lost is par for the course,
Racing to the finish line.

Travel can be hazardous,
A flat tire losing air, picked up a nail,
A printer out of paper collecting dust,
Rock chips and dead insects,
Loss of memory and lack of imagination,
Cracks in the windshield,
Diminished vision.
Am I running out of gas,
Coasting downhill in neutral,
Just around the corner
From the last service station,
A block away from writer's block.

Exhilarating to get refueled,
Finally accelerating mile after mile,
Burn rubber and go full throttle,
Find my place in the last winner's circle,
A faster track that I can create,
Trying not to lose control,
As easy as a blank sheet of paper,
And turning on the ignition one last time,
Adjusting the rear-view mirror
To view the past
And cruise control into the future.

Literary Criticism

Interpret the life out of this poem
Analyze it to death
Work it and work it to no end
Alter its breadth and its depth

Expand what the poet intended
Find typos and incomplete thoughts
Explore innuendos and meanings
That clearly had never been wrought

Publish your thesis in journals
Seek higher acclaim from your peers
And bask in the glory eternal
Where false perceptions are reared

Finally

For the past two months or more,
I have been sending poems for publication,
With eighty-six poems
Spread across my office floor.
The dog walks on them asking to be fed
On the ground where I have spent a thousand hours
Writing out of a vacuum
In order to make fifty bucks
And two copies of some magazine's latest issue.

Well here it is,
It finally happened,
Some editors were intrigued
And resonated with my talent.
They are all published and well renowned
Have all been here before,
Wondering why they are writing poetry
And if they have an audience,
And why they are still reading this poem.

Yes, this one has been accepted,
Even with my doggerel and sarcasm,
Lack of poetic imagery and style,
Void of ingenuity and deeper meaning.
After having read previous editions
And conformed to the guidelines,
Relegated to submission,
This meager poem avoided rejection
And the obligatory form letter.

If you are looking for some depth here,
You will have to provide it yourself,
Possibly someone struggling to be successful,
Trying to have his voice heard and understood,
Persevering and never giving up,
Like someone jumping out of an airplane
And discovering that the main shoot doesn't open.
Release the shoot and punch the reserve shoot,
And if that doesn't open what do you do,
You keep punching,
And what do you do if it still doesn't open,
You keep punching.
Now that's an image for you.

The Kiss of the Sixties

Spin the bottle was no longer a game of chance
The consequences more dire now in junior high
The days of Viola Wolf's social dancing class were over
The cha-cha and cherry cokes at Mayhew's
Fizzled out with the onset of turning thirteen
And realizing that things were not quite the same.

A Bar Mitzvah heralded becoming a man
A memorized Torah portion proclaimed the triumph
Whatever the chant meant it was good to get through it
With only one Hebrew word mispronounced
And only one day to grow up.

The sixties transformed my teenage years
The crew cut grew to shoulder length
Free love was never really free
A Nehru jacket and wire-rimmed glasses
Helped me see the peace signs
And understand Bob Dylan and the Beatles.

I really wanted to make love not war
If I wore a bra I would have burned it
I watched Lee Harvey Oswald get shot on TV
Thinking that I could really ban the bomb
And end the war in Viet Nam
Move to Bohemia and wear some beads.

I knew flower children who took the pill
Wore bell bottoms and tie-dyed tee shirts
Face paint was not my way to get high
Though I learned how to roll a pretty tight joint
Burn incense and chant anti-establishment slogans
Avoid the draft as best I could.

The wind always smelled like it was stoned
And my bottled emotions were as high as a dove
I took my first steps on the moon
And protested in peaceful bewilderment
Adolescence had smudged white lipstick on my cheek
Taught me how to grow up and speak my peace.

Marijuana Melody

The grass in Acapulco was gold,
And became more cultivated
In midtown Manhattan
Where it lived in plastic bags,
Frequented all the joints and high rises,
As was the latest fashion.

Smart ones smoked dope,
Which was kind of ironic,
Took their hits but not alone,
Had a toke before a movie,
Everyone was feeling groovy,
Everyone was getting stoned.

You could smell it in the air,
Always knew when it was there,
Permeating like a pungent breeze,
Laughing like the joy of scent,
A good feeling of euphoria,
And a bad case of the munchies.

A hippie shared a bong without hesitation,
Hookah and water pipe for filtration,
Transformed the fire into a burning cough,

An intravenous gasping iron lung.
Pass the roach and hold your breath,
Turn you on and get you off.

Back then it was clandestine,
A secret that everyone knew,
Today at the dispensary,
You can choose the best for you,
A flower that fulfills your mood,
Like going to a pharmacy.

Do you want peace and quiet,
Something calm to go to sleep,
Or just want to feel incredible,
An ointment for your back pain,
A tincture for high anxiety and depression,
Have you thought about an edible?

The rules and laws are finally changing,
The mellow party has just begun,
An appropriate time to entertain,
Get high and dial up a little fun,
Introduce all the guests with cordiality,
And welcome without formality, Mary Jane.

Karma

Hitchhiking south from Santa Rosa,
Stopping to drink a Coca-Cola,
Into the mountains past Monterey,
Forty-five miles to Tassajara.

Where Zen baths flow and hot springs run,
Daily meditations set the tone,
No breeze coming from the bay,
The ashram filled with everyone.

Counting breaths for forty-five minutes,
Cross-legged lotus with eager students,
And ancient monks, heads shaved,
Barely moving doing their business.

A bell rings clearly for time to walk
In circles around, no one talks,
And then back to the same cushion saved,
Round two clears the mind of paradox.

For breakfast boiled eggs and pickles,
A fly was on my lips that tickled,
But I left it there consciously,
Lapping the salty sweat that trickled.

Clean the cabin a straw broom sweeps,
One of the monks is still asleep,
Work for the day is boxing dried pears,
That had cured in the sun for a week.

Another *zazen* before vegetarian dinner,
I was starting to feel a bit thinner,
I chose to get hit with a stick on the shoulder
To better focus as a beginner.

Soup, rice, vegetables, and tea,
Everyone appeared hungry casually,
Nestled in the mountains between boulders,
Stars shining passionately.

Another morning silence espoused,
Breakfast on tables with mung bean sprouts,
My work to scrape calcium off of the rocks,
Fortuitously in the ladies' bathhouse.

A female monk with head shaved,
Was offered the exotic tea she craved,
Blew into the spout, knocked off the lid,
Her spirit was not very well behaved.

Another monk was more in a fit,
He could not handle the day-to-day grit,
He said, "I'm going to San Francisco,
I need a break from this Zen shit."

Three more days and I hit the road,
Really nothing left on my mind to unload,
I had reached where I needed to go,
In time for the next consequential episode.

No Hippies Allowed

The war on drugs had just said, "No,"
And a handwritten sign posted on Sanibel Island
Threatened to restrict every Volkswagen van,
Block those who did not fit the mold,
Who just wanted some beach, a parcel of paradise,
Like the sea turtles that came to hatch their eggs
Below the tide, close to the Gulf of Mexico.

A threatened fragment of society had created labels
To manifest hostility in the warm sand,
Where the rangers searched with flashlights
And long-haired campers pitched tents,
Lit small fires for ambience,
Ate dried fruits and nuts,
And peacefully explored the stars for reasons.

I Wish I Were Not Dead

People walk by and say prayers,
I haven't seen some of them in years,
I wonder why they think they have to visit
This ritual service, I would prefer to miss it.

My life ended much too abruptly,
I needed some time to finish up,
The list I recently wrote of several pages,
To get it done would have taken me ages.

I thought that I was pretty well alive,
Vital, vibrant, and thriving,
My pulse and pressure always strong,
Not ready for the swan's melancholic song.

I did not need to be released,
And join those previously deceased,
Things were going fine, securely,
This all happened prematurely.

Who made the decision I had to go,
Who do they think they are I'd like to know,
Could they take it back, moreover,
I'd like to have a do-over.

But now that I'm gone, I need to tell
That there's no such thing as Heaven and Hell,
Someone made that up a long time ago,
You'll have to wait for your time to know.

As for me, I'll have to make do,
And discover what's now in plain view,
Enjoy the environs of this new myth,
Relieved of the things that I would normally deal with.

So, take this message from the grave,
Try your hardest to be brave,
No reason for you to tearfully lament,
Take a deep breath and savor every moment.

Reborn as a Javelina

Roaming the Arizona desert in a small herd,
sharpening my tusks,
scouring for prickly pear cactus, lizards,
and other creatures of the night,
I remember that I used to have a cell phone
and an IP address,
could make Zoom calls with my friends,
and go to Safeway to buy meat and fresh veggies.

Now I am writing poems early in the morning
about reincarnation,
what will I be next,
what would I want to be,
what wouldn't I want to be.

When I was a young javelina,
my wild javelina buddies
would ask if I believed in reincarnation.
Of course I did, duh,
but I never told them
that I could speak English,
a little French, Spanish, and Chinese,
loved corned beef,
had Googled on Safari,
and was afraid of javelinas.

My obnoxious pals also ask
if I were to be reincarnated
what I would like to be.
Certainly not a human,
been there done that,
For now, I just want enough shade,
a little peace and quiet,
and a glass of cold water.

When Parents Die

The obituary reads that they died peacefully
at home surrounded by loved ones,
but we know that didn't actually happen.
Some of the family don't get along,
haven't seen each other in years,
estranged or disowned, struggling
in the distance and counting their inheritance.

The cause of death is never old age,
as old age brings complications with it.
The heart has worn out like a hand
that can no longer make a fist,
has lost its punch, its dexterity,
along with the brain
that is no longer connecting
to the network,
misfiring on cylinders
that are overheated,
unable to produce any power.

The deathbed is dusty,
like ashes to ashes,
has a musty odor of old sheets
that haven't been changed,
and a pillow that hasn't been turned.

There is no relief
in not having to call the doctor again,
as the necessary paperwork
requires a signature for every emotion
while the celebration of life unfolds,
the photographs mounted on poster board,
the food ordered
and arrangements made
that take your mind away
from where it wants to grieve silently alone.

We will be there one of these days,
off in our own world
and remembering their last words,
"I've said everything I need to say,
I've said everything already,
many times,
there's nothing else."

An Open Bed in Memory Care

He couldn't remember what he had for lunch,
but knew all the streets in Port-au-Prince
from fifty years ago,
could describe them in vivid detail
to his Haitian daytime caregiver.

Management at Forest Trace Senior Living
took the air out of the tires
of his silver Buick Regal
so that he wouldn't try to drive
to the hospital to see his wife,
recovering from a stroke.
He called AAA to get them inflated,
drove to Firestone and bought new ones.

The Health Administrator
said that he fit right in at the Alzheimer's facility,
with comfort dogs roaming freely from room to room
and a crazy woman trying to steal his clothes
stuffed in an old wooden dresser.

My last visit right after I sold his car,
talked with his doctor
about discontinuing blood transfusions.
The doctor used the term *compos mentis*,
referring to my mother,
and as an only child,
I had to make the call
of where to go from here.

He was having dessert,
a chocolate brownie that he thought too gooey,
and asked if he had a heart attack.
I said our last good-bye with a kiss
and sat in the driver's seat
of a rental car and watched a nighthawk fly
high in the sky and eventually out of sight.

Hanging On

Too many people have died,
    fallen off sheer cliffs,
looking down an artesian well
    past the frogs floating
unable to escape stone walls,
    sink holes in the pavement,
suspension bridges collapsing,
    people falling into chasms,
planning what they will have for dinner,
    if they are going to have enough to eat,
share their meal with hungry children
    wallowing like tadpoles in the street.

Weddings and funerals are now allowed
    as long as they don't draw a crowd,
dead bodies in masks join the procession
    and vow to honor and obey,
brides draped in sheer white lace,
    veiled from anything they will see today,
images of nursing homes and parlors,
    arthritic hands grasping in the air,
wondering if there is anybody there,
    anyone who cares who really cares,
they need to tidy up all their affairs
bequeath possessions to their heirs.

Children watch grandparents fade away,
	pay their bills and bring them photos,
show them what the world is like,
	fill prescriptions to climb a mountain,
that last journey without delay,
	boulders to never be rappelled,
life support to be withheld,
	the anchor points now within reach,
an altitude at the end of the rope,
	with an attitude to be released,
they fall into the sky,
	live in memory and never die.

Holding on, too many people are suspended,
	sinking deeper into a depression,
watching life events on faded calendars
	and walking step by step in silent procession,
living life day to day seems to be the only way,
	the only option to break the fast of night,
arriving to hear resounding bells
	and prepare the liturgy for somber last rites,
yet the bells can bring some light to life,
	exuberance that comes as a bright surprise,
reveling in a host of unencumbered moments,
	those rare ecstatic times to memorialize.

Phantasmagoria

Ghosts and UFOs are back.
If you listen closely, you can hear them,
Can see them in the house and overhead.
Their sounds are totally different,
Nothing that you have ever heard before,
Resembling what electricity sounds like,
The invisible secret souls of science.

The naked eye can make something out of nothing,
Ghouls and goblins coming out of the woodwork,
Phantoms haunting those who are vulnerable
To hearing voices and seeing apparitions.
Our fascination with the supernatural is chilling,
Witches, warlocks, and mysterious spirits,
Demons tormenting the children of innocent children.

The aliens are also waiting in the wings,
Flying in the skies at night.
They land in the cinema for our fascination,
As we project ourselves into other worlds,
That are not even worlds or science fiction.
Light years away they play the roles we write for them,
Exploding like stars dancing in our mind
And keeping us alert to every possibility.

Has this been going on forever, pursuit of the unfathomable,
This questioning about self- induced hallucination?
Why do we wonder what is real and what is not,
What is ephemeral and what is beyond possible?
When you hear those migrant ghosts
And see those luminescent UFOs,
You cannot help but stop and reflect
Was that just something there or in my head,
Was my chemistry unbalanced, my electricity short circuited?
Look into every corner to make sure you are not alone,
And try to figure out what is known about the unknown.

In a Trance

Walking from room to room
In and out of different doorways
Remembering what there is left to remember
And forgetting details of what might have happened.
Muted voices talk as if in dreams
Appear and disappear at will
Putting one foot forward in front of the other
And not going anywhere in particular.
Everything learned no longer matters
As nothing is not really real
And everything is nothing in the shade
Faded light and intermittent darkness.
No one is at home and numbness pervades
No sound or direction in the haze
A quiet empty void of emptiness prevails.
Open your eyes and see what you can see
Blink several times to make sure it is real
Reach out and touch every breath
The vapors and the whiffs of solitude
Windows to what lies before you
Before returning to the dimness if not darkness
A light wash on a not so empty canvas.

The Chihuly Museum

I thought about a poem as a collection of words put in a particular order, and I questioned what if the order were sorted in the same way that a deck of fifty-two cards is shuffled. So, I wrote a fifty-two-word poem about Chihuly Garden and Glass in Seattle and put it into a computerized word shuffler three times. Each of the three new versions was put into poetic lines and minimally modified.

Flowers blown from colored glass adorn gardens
Of crystal spires sprouting majestically from the fertile ground
And showering fuchsia, heliotrope, pink, and gold lights
Across the museum floor, spiraling around each other
In spectacular folds of delight and illuminating
The throngs of tourists to The Emerald City
Gazing in awe and disbelief.

i.

Tourists and spires sprouting glass from the ground
And from emerald that others adorn
Spiraling across flowers in awe from fuchsia
Crystal gardens illuminating the fertile spectacular colored floor
Each gazing in city delight
Showering heliotrope the museum with pink folds of light
In and around throngs of gold disbelief majestically blown.

ii.

Heliotrope from the spectacular museum sprouting delight
Spiraling flowers and disbelief illuminating majestically for the gazing
Each around the garden's fuchsia fertile city in the floor
Awe across pink throngs of gold spires of tourists
Crystals adorn lights and other colors fold
From the glass emerald showering in the ground blown.

iii.

From in the glass awe of gold gardens
Tourists to emerald lights are blown
In the sprouting of flowers fold spectacular fertile heliotrope
Others showering from around majestically
The city illuminating across delight
Gazing and spiraling to the crystal throngs the floor fuchsia
Museum spires in disbelief each ground colored pink adorn.

A Perfect Square

Everything can be written and carefully drawn equal like all men and women with each side equal to every other side all lined up neatly and perfectly straight as an arrow and tucked in tightly like hospital corners and picture frames all horizontal with ninety degree angles distinctly marking all of the intersections measured with left turns and right turns everyone having more than one turn that allows all of the pedestrians unlimited access to their right of way and a variety of inalienable rights allowing them to cross the stream of consciousness and reach the other side where nothing is crooked bent or at an angle that they are not able to navigate or easily climb a set of stairs with handrails and climbing holds that follow one another and routes that lead them to a kind of symmetrical perfection and the realization of all of their dreams and aspirations avoiding detours or deviations just a clear path that they can follow and assume a posture that they can fight any obstacle along the way and be on offense and defense all at the same time no matter where they are or where they have been or where they are going but always ready prepared for action and full of life well-rehearsed and practiced trained for every event and anxious to get started and get going get on with it moving forward with all of their inner strength and ability and agility hopeful and self-assured and yet spontaneous they spring to life side by side and bound into the fertile ground of opportunity refreshed and rejuvenated and ready to show the world who they are and what they are all about figures of perfection in their own right equal and different like a square with sides of air and angles that are not always there but always present like fingers running through your hair a hidden strength that crosses the street with other men and women and meets you side by side in this square.

Epilogue

"...approach thy grave, like one who wraps the drapery of
his couch about him, and lies down to pleasant dreams."
                              from "Thanatopsis," William Cullen Bryant

I write my will over and over,
Every day a new way to leave behind
All that I am apparently worth,
Memorabilia, victories and defeats,
As I limp, grunt, and gasp with old age,
Unfilled prescriptions, unfulfilled aspirations.

My attorney charges a fee to prepare it succinctly
Into an immortal estate binder,
Like an embalmed body in a vinyl coffin,
With legal language that avoids probate,
Hereafter desires that will rise from the tomb
To bloom silently cold in the great unknown moonlight.

The pen I use to sign this final directive,
Almost out of ink like a last breath,
Attempts to spell a semblance of meaning.
No more codicils to notarize,
This testament tries to die honestly
Without fanfare, living in trust.

Executing this instrument on the near side of death,
I appear to be of sound mind and memory,
Not acting under duress, menace, fraud,
Undue influence, misrepresentation, or frivolity.

Just give me a clean exit, let me rest alone in peace,
Distribute all my property, extinguish all the paperwork,
Everything bequeathed to my beneficiaries,
So that they can write their wills
With less than solemn ceremony,
Again and again and again,
And look forward to sharing the inevitable destination
And ultimate resolution of life.

II

Form Maladies

Dear Family and Friends

i.   Alas, a Shakespearean sonnet

Alas, this year has gone into the mist.
I must have missed the meaning of each month.
And whilst I tried to figure out the gist,
I never got it right, not even once.
In vain, I sorted through the days and weeks,
The dates and hours that measured each event.
Yet, recollecting all the stops and streaks,
I could not find a time that was well spent.
A scurry here, a flurry there, for sure,
Haphazard moments interspersed in space,
A list of things as pointless to ignore
As aches and pains that always found their place.
And yet, I sense, I'm just as devious,
As when I started the year previous.

ii.   Still Nagging, a Petrarchan sonnet

On second thought, I have more nagging smarts,
They come and go like splinters on the skin,
As some from me and others from my kin,
Will show their ugly heads in fits and starts.

Rotator cuffs and other body parts,
Herniated discs, boils on my chin,
Ankles put together with screw and pin,
Heart arrhythmia, my medical charts.
Yet, I'm saved from osteoarthritis,
Can run a mile with unstrained nimble pace,
Not a hint of planar fasciitis.
I sing and speak my mind
And never have to deal with laryngitis.

iii.   Lately, a Petrarchan sonnet

Of late, I've seen the doctor more than once
With aches and pains profound from head to toe.
I've had diseases you should never know
And suffered them with whimpers, moans, and grunts.
Colonoscopies, coronary stunts,
Migraine headaches, influenza stole the show,
Total knee replacement a month ago,
Heartburn, catheters, and surgical shunts.
Basal-cell carcinoma and stiff neck,
Erectile dysfunction and swollen glands,
Plugged ears, ingrown toenails I've had seven.
My body presents as a total wreck
From gingivitis to arthritic hands.
At least I am not pregnant, thank heaven.

To Get a Shot or Not?
a Shakespearian sonnet

"That is the question." Hamlet

If Shakespeare had written this rhymed sonnet,
He would have penned this year's aberration
As a tragedy, you can count on it,
A poem needing immunization.
Now I look forward to a decision,
With Pfizer or Moderna to proceed,
To get vaccinated with precision
And immunized from COVID at warp speed.
Do I roll up my sleeve and take the risk,
Trusting the Center for Disease Control,
That their needle's injection will be brisk,
And the virologists achieve their goal?
Perhaps I can emerge from this abyss,
Remove my mask and give my wife a kiss.

Two Lives, a Spenserian sonnet

Her life has joined with mine, at times the two
Have been as one, a union of two minds
And hearts that shared soft sounds we never knew,
The moments that companionship defines.
Her beauty in my reaching arms reclines
And speaks in tones that flutter in the air
Unwritten thoughts not captured in these lines
That curl around the whispers in her hair.
She knows I wish that she were always there,
Forever in this dream that we have made.
To be removed would simply be unfair
And cast for good our laughs and tears in shade.
Today is our forever hand in hand
For future days we cannot understand.

Rights and Wrongs, a Miltonic sonnet

The Bill of Rights adds the ten amendments
To our Constitution, asserts free speech,
Freedom of religion allowed for each,
The press to tell truth with independence.
The right to bear arms for all descendants,
Laws permit machine guns within our reach,
Criminals and counsel due process preach.
Legal controversy and resentments
That appear in court remain debated
Before grand juries trying to impress
And tell free people how they have to act.
So, no wonder we are not elated
With ruthless politicians in distress
Unable to distinguish fake from fact.

Sherman's Deli, a *terza rima* sonnet

The crowd out front had corned beef on their mind,
Sliced pastrami piled high on Jewish rye,
The deli scene unruly and yet kind.

Large nova platters not in short supply,
Potato kugel, latkes, a huge choice,
Matzoh ball soup that no one can deny.

The customers who come to feast rejoice,
Observe their culinary tradition,
Remember old delis and raise their voice.

Half sour pickles a fine addition
To go with bagels, brisket, and challah,
Some cheesecake, who cares about nutrition?

A chocolate egg cream, Cel-Ray, rugelach,
No wonder we are all *mashugana.*

To the Lake

Eugene Macintyre Erwin
November 16, 1913 - April 15, 1997

The elk can go up the mountain now,
To the top where the air breathes freely.
Winter has turned its relentless course,
Cleared its lungs of cold and frozen dreams
And opened calmly into a realm between journeys.

A peaceful warrior, a twinkle in his eye,
Marches to the lake.

Now the deer range freely in the Okanogan forest,
Grazing on the seeds of new life blown from Concunully to Chesaw.
The chest of the earth has settled into a steady rhythm,
Gone are the struggles, the twisted paths of detail,
And here are the moments that give life its meaning.

A peaceful warrior, with his boots on,
Marches to the lake.

For a while, the world seems to stop, knowing where he is going—
The peasants on the Burma Road, past presidents and military leaders,
Hunters in Sitka and Ketchikan, cruise ships on the Panama Canal,

Skiers at Squaw Valley, salmon at Spee-bi-dah,
Vegetables in the garden, cousins pegging on their cribbage boards—
All know that he will get there.

The three daughters of the wind hold their breath,
Watch him leave for Sidley Lake.

He chooses the road and records his every step,
Sets his course and measures a steady stride.
The marathon is his to reach his goal,
To dance again with his lovely bride.

And a choir of wildflowers
Will open to the sun and sing;
With peace and joy, we'll see you in the spring—
"I'll see you in the spring."

Talking to the Ashes

Evelyn Rosetsky Lyon, February 23, 1915 – January 29, 2002
Joel Croner Lyon, November 3, 1910 – November 30, 1997

The Queen has died.
Her impatient pleas to let her go
Have been answered.
The Atlantic and the Pacific
Have sent their final waves good-bye.
The doormen at the Normandy
And the snowbirds of Inverrary
Observe a moment of silence.

You have rested peacefully in my closet
These past four years sleeping with the photo albums,
Singing *Old Man River,* dreaming of New York steaks,
A hole-in-one and sharing your severed thumb trick.
"Are you a little easier now?" you asked
Repeatedly, not remembering,
Tangled in thoughts of stock and bond markets,
A '54 Chrysler, hands of gin rummy,
Electric shavers, peppermint hard candies,
Corrugated boxes, plastic bags,
Looking in the obituary column to see if you were there.

"Easier than what?" she said, and remembered
Removing my splinters from the boardwalk at Ocean Gate,
Crocheting Afghans and baking Chicken Kiev,
The intricate weave of Manhattan buses and subways,
Flying in turbulence, living in moderation,
When she brought you to our wedding in Aspen
With *schmaltz* to make chopped liver,
The scent of Indian curry in hospice,
White chocolate syrup drizzled on morphine.
Yes, much easier.

We transformed emergency rooms
And taught doctors about depression and desire.
We celebrated suffering as best we could,
With bagels and Nova, Mogen David and matzah ball soup.
Although she found comfort in every phone call,
The taste of ten-ingredient chow mein,
She was impatient and ready to abandon the struggle.
"Let me go," she told the rabbi,
"Take me already."
We listened because she was the Queen.

The world has changed from Brooklyn to Philly,
And the prayers and meditations are now for you,
Yisgadal v'yiskadash sh'me rabbo...
You will always be together
Scattered in a world that knows eternity.
The clam chowder has just the right amount of clams,
Not too rubbery, and not too many potatoes.
Soar above the Okanagan valley,
Dance beyond the Enderby cliffs,
And live like there is no tomorrow.

Good Shepherd Family Home

Cynthia Ann Henderson
February 12, 1947 – November 3, 2018

The caregivers from the Philippines
Smile, cook and clean.
They share their stories in Tagalog,
Shuffling slowly from room to room,
Servants to the end of life.

Soon the opposing forces of the universe will quiet down,
The room will not be too hot or too cold,
The bed not too hard or too soft,
No sound, no smell, just lifeless paintings on the wall,
Flowers asleep in their vase,
A fan no longer stirring the air.

The poets have tried to capture the moment
As the poem searches for words,
Nothing eloquent, nothing profound,
Yet something we will all embrace,
Like it or not, we will all be there
With every religion, with every prayer and psalm.
With every hymn and eulogy,
We will enter the room alone but not alone.

We cannot make sense of this,
A husband walking around the marina
Imagining trimmed sailboats from the past
That now have little wind in their sails,
Only memories blowing in the breeze
And conjuring up thoughts of distant days.

Two sisters capture life with open arms,
Pave the way at home for an eternity,
Understanding that the pain and suffering
Will no longer rule the seas
Where longed for peace and tranquility
Will be the new order in the final bedroom.
No more days and nights,
No more attempts to explain and answer questions,
No more waking up and going to sleep,
Surrounded by love, a just death, simple, pure and clean.

Shimshon

August 14, 2007 – March 31, 2015

"Please remember me and please strengthen me
just this time that I may at once be avenged."
Judges 16:29-30

Our cat died this morning. I bought some tulips,
I couldn't arrange them yellow, red, and white.
Ikebana would not connect heaven, man, and earth—
No way to make them look quite right.
We found a vase in the laundry room,
Ordered a small wooden box for his ashes.
Lymphoma a large word for a lively black cat.

I bought an apple fritter to celebrate his life,
Seven and a half years avenging himself every morning,
Sitting beside the computer disturbing my papers,
Pushing my pen, sunbathing under the desk lamp.
The prognosis not good, maybe a couple of months,
Intestinal surgery, chemotherapy and vet bills.
The flowers on sale, the doughnut under a dollar,
How do you know what to do when a pet dies?

A Bombay, could jump six feet high, retrieve plush toys,
Enjoy Fancy Feast savory salmon and empty tuna cans.
Meow Cat Rescue hailed him Chief, a ruler in charge.
We later renamed him Shimshon for Samson, after our Jerusalem guide.
A pillar of strength, performed heroic feats
In every drawer bag and box, in every closet shelf and cupboard,
Under foot, in control, and always present.
He chose when to lose his life.

My wife wanted to know what was wrong
In the family room on the floor in front of the television.
No picture, no sound between earth and heaven
The fireplace off, no flames, no warmth, no light.
Death does not compute, does not guide, is not on sale.
Winnie, our domestic lynx, his litter mate sister,
Stopped suddenly at him lying there, knew that he had fallen,
And hid under the bed.

Winnie Went to Sleep

August 14, 2007 – September 28, 2020

Her remains came from Loyal Companion
In a cedar box for our Pacific Northwest girl.
We had a choice of three containers.
Medications could not detain her.
They also sent her paw print and some hair,
A certificate that she is no longer here.

A packet of flower seeds for a beloved friend,
And tips on coping with the loss of a pet.
She would rather have a can of food,
Jump up on the bed, onto my chest,
Close her eyes and have a little rest.

She lost a lot of weight in her last days,
Talked to us and kept us calm,
Walked from room to room, to special places,
Found a ray of sunlight to stay warm,
Slept on pillows, a cat bed by the fireplace.

In her cedar box she sleeps in the family room,
Perched on a table with a full view
Of everything we say and everything we do.
Just as before, we are in her care.
She is still here.

The Courtyard, a glosa

> "Because I could not stop for Death –
> He kindly stopped for me –
> The Carriage held but just Ourselves –
> And immortality."

> from Emily Dickinson, "479"

Meyer lemons in abundance given to housekeepers
Every other week as they dust the fans and vacuum the casita,
The gardener gets a bag on Saturdays, mows the lawn, trims bougainvilleas.
Epicurious has a lemon bar recipe dusted with powdered sugar
For all who enter the bungalow and comment about the tree,
Greeting me with, "Buenos dias" as is their shibboleth,
We are here at least for now, a short time,
To visit and open my gate along with a neighbor
Who always brings strawberries, when asked why, says out of breath,
"Because I could not stop for Death –"

Everyone crosses the red Rubicon parked in the driveway,
Observes the pink powder puff that climbs and sprawls along the wall,
Ceramic pottery from Guadalajara that paints the story
Of La Catrina, the sacred symbol of the afterlife,
Enjoying every day despite the sporadic haboob,
While also embracing death in the desert winds that portend inevitable reality.
Smooth agaves line the walkway, tropical and succulent, spiky and spiny,

As I wait for one last letter, ominous news from the mailman driving by,
I signal to him to deliver the final message and set me free,
He kindly stopped for me –

I walk now with measured twilight into the courtyard,
The pathway a transition lined with California Gold
Bought from the quarry at Southwest Boulder and Stone.
The cactus garden prepares for sleep, tired after all these years,
Like centuries of endless conversation.
The neighbors sobbed, could not control themselves
As I boarded my wagon on the eternal caravan,
Took my seat next to Life and Death.
Time had stored me on its shelves,
The Carriage held but just Ourselves –

No River Styx to ferry across, just normal departure with little fanfare
From the gentlemen and ladies going to Hades,
No elation nor despair, like water changing from solid to liquid to gas,
Like ashes to ashes, this too shall pass as I pass,
And soon I will be welcomed into the house I created,
Dust will cover the lemons powdered with spirituality,
La Catrina will embrace me and say, "Buenas noches."
I am at peace as I step over the threshold,
Open the door, and let myself in to the vacuum of finality,
And immortality.

Searching for God

A Golden Shovel after Mick Jagger and Keith Richards'
"You Can't Always Get What You Want"

The price of pine nuts now so expensive I
can't afford to buy luxuries anymore as I saw
that eggs have gone up butter flour lettuce potatoes even her
coffee costs so much more today
soon I won't be able to eat or drink at
all restaurants closing daily understaffed so that the
sense of loss as I grow older receives unwelcome reception

Eternal life is not around the corner with a
promise that I could make a toast and lift a glass
of immortal champagne of hope and prosperity of
aging gracefully everlasting with wine
and roses even a bowl of cherries more expensive in
every store and every corner and I tell her
that we will be fine will get there just hold my hand

Together can find our way she and I
drifting in an era that no one knew
would turn out this way no guarantees as she
would always say when we first met and would
wonder if we'd ever argue about what or anything and meet
every night after the longest day she let me hold her
quietly in my arms and make a connection

We've lived a life long enough at
various destinations and vacations that brought her
happiness and exaltation at beaches with our feet
in the sand while watching the sunset was
a serene way to close the day and tell her
that tomorrow with the sunrise we'll be footloose
in our journey as woman and man

Accepting all challenges with resolve and no
hesitation looking for meaning and seeking reasons why you
are here why we found each other and if destiny can't
explain what this is about forever and ever and always
from the very beginning until now we still get
to absorb sunshine and the power of nature with what
senses we have that tell me and you
that this heaven on earth is all that we really want

Water and air resplendent right in front of you
no reason to look elsewhere or say that you can't
find spirituality and soulfulness always
present to be discovered within ourselves as we get
on with our lives exploring what
is before our open eyes and realizing that you
and I have everything and nothing else that we could possibly want

I clip coupons from the newspaper pine nuts on sale but
every day we have to fix something if
we want to maintain our home that you
have gradually built and decorated as we try
and try again as we once did sometime
long ago and just yesterday where you'll
shop around discover bargains and wonders looking to find

Beauty in the journey until the destination you
seek reaches out and touches us so that we get
ultimate fulfillment in every moment and finally shows us what
this supreme adventure is all about and that you
and I can live every day celebrating the joy that we really need

Autobiography of a Poem, free verse

"Poetry is the spontaneous overflow of powerful feelings: it
takes its origin from emotion recollected in tranquility."

William Wordsworth

In third grade, Mrs. Mayberry had us write a poem every day.
It became ritual at Hunter College Elementary.
One of mine was published in the 8-9 Y Literary Journal.
Blue ink on a mimeograph
Discovered in a box several years ago.
I wish I still had it, something about feet or shoes,
Three lines with rhymes, very elementary.
She read a poem to the class daily,
My formal introduction to poetry.

Master Wiessler taught poems in 11th grade.
His lesson plan at McBurney Prep
Connected to the YMCA on 63rd between Central Park and Broadway.
I remember William Wordsworth,
Lines Composed a Few Miles above Tintern Abbey,
"The heavy and the weary weight
of all this unintelligible world is lightened,"
Difficult for me to relate to
The words that united meaning and sound.
Not really prepared, I started writing poems again that year.

At first my poems came out of the emotion
Of feeling sad about something—
Relationships broken, loss of friendships, something gone wrong,
A way to express feelings of failure privately.
I wrote an essay for homework about love.
Wiessler commented, "nihilistic."
But I kept writing poems.
If I had a poem, then things were not that bad.
At least I had a poem.

Most of the early poems were not kept for long
Nor shared with anyone, mine alone.
This author had no audience
Until I started saving them.
Something about poetry was
Like music, nature's rhythm, dancing with rhymes,
Ideas and images that voiced themselves,
Tempo and meter asking for interpretation,
Statements that came out of a nowhere somewhere.

I met Gail Davis at a rodeo in Madison Square Garden
And later wrote the terrible poem, *I Dream of Annie,*
"White leather tassels and diamond studded Stetson,
Ivory handled twin six-shooters...
That have shot holes in a thousand aces."
She autographed her glossy photo for me
And called me by the wrong name.
So, I reflected on the embarrassment
And at least I had a poem.

In college I read original poems on a makeshift stage at The Pendulum
Attending CCT in Potsdam. Everyone was stoned.
My escape from engineering and mathematics—
Writing and directing *Pandora Experimentia*,
Wes Craven's first film behind the camera.
I did all I could do to graduate
And move on to something more creative.
My '64 Chevy Impala was totaled in the snow in front of Wes's house.
I had to take an Amtrak to Baltimore, Johns Hopkins, Elliot Coleman.

Three days living with the Jesuits
Until I found a third-floor row house apartment.
I read poems when I woke up, T.S. Eliot's
The Love Song of J. Alfred Prufrock,
"I have heard the mermaids singing, each to each."
I was writing a poem almost every day.

Took a manuscript over winter break to Random House.
Submitted it with a cover letter, walked to the elevator.
The door opened and there was Bennett Cerf.
I should have introduced myself but
He walked out and I walked in.
Creating metaphors and similes, playing around with words
I learned all the terms, experimented and emulated,
Form, function, and purpose all intertwined, structured and free,
Art and design following one another, not really one before the other.

So now to warm up I choose various forms,
Give myself assignments in tranquility.
I try to develop some discipline

And be creative along the way.
Searching through rhymes and synonyms,
Universal meanings that wake me up in the night;
Not always flowery, not always serious.
If I have a poem, at least I have a poem
And things are not that bad.

Drawing a Blank, blank verse

Paralysis controls the empty thoughts
Defies attempts to break out of the dark
What purpose tries to fill the empty page
And shed some light on what it means to be
The themes have all been told a million times
The details changed to sound a current song
What melody can rise above the rest
Can break the mold and sing another verse
To those who do not understand this thing
Or try to read between the lines of hope
The message is obscured in daily tasks
And never seems to rise above the heat
Yet poets try to find their time to write
Alone and in the quiet cave of calm
They mumble to themselves to hear the sound
Again and yet again to make it right
In desperation they will find a way
And figure out how they can speak their mind
Avoid cliché and rhymes that never work
Their job to bring the reader in the room
Or keep the poem under key a while
To let it grow and turn into itself
A work of art internal as the blood
Of artists painting figures in the dark

To capture meaning in the slightest stroke
The words are pounded out a world apart
They join themselves as if they never met
And when they do they look into their eyes
And try to find some meaning in a blink
The portal to the soul is bare and free
Inviting those who wish to venture in
Rejecting those who cannot find their way
Yet once inside the search is not complete
It never is it only replicates
The past that came before a distant time
A future wish that sits upon the shelf
With all the other books that someone wrote
And dared to show itself before the world
Could find the time to wrap it in some cloth
So you wonder what you should do now
You came this far and now completely lost
The message convoluted in the scheme
Of iambs strung together some by chance
With others hanging deftly by a thread
A meter like a wave pretends to crest
And crashes to the shore within your brain
You say you have to leave so go ahead
It does not matter what you choose to do
You can forget this meeting all at once
Or take it with you for another time
A rhyme will surely help you disappear
Will transport you into the atmosphere
Surprise you cannot get away so fast
The drama continues ad nauseum

The ending was false the buildup fake
A rondo with no flourish annoying
Your hopes were up but that was all your fault
The game continues puts your dreams to shame
A tragedy for you who wants a break
The humor of the moment needs to grow
Find something fun to lighten up the mood
But weary of pentameter gone long
There is no way to write a funny line
So hand in hand we amble in the dark
You curse that you have ever started this
And now that I am stuck to find an end
It's up to you to figure out what's next

My Mystic Rhyming Muse, a sestina

Where do you find your words?
Poems in your sleep
Inspiration and creation a mystery
Or a thesaurus
Rhyming dictionary
Exceptionally mysterious

Less serious than mysterious
Passwords and poets provide your words
More cautionary than a dictionary
Keep writing as you sleep
A chorus sings inside your thesaurus
A fun epiphany for this mystery

You have history with this mystery
More imperious than mysterious
Don't ignore us with your thesaurus
Be absurd searching for the words
Knee-deep thoughts interrupt sleep
More contrary than a regular dictionary

Certainly more fragmentary than the dictionary
More blistery than any mystery
Skin-deep in sleep
Glorious thoughts that become mysterious
Revisions afterwards that substitute new words
Like a tyrannosaurus gobbling up a thesaurus

Aurora Borealis lights up your thesaurus
With exemplary choices from the dictionary
Like migrating birds the season brings words
A symphony of mystery
Nothing deleterious just simply mysterious
Multiple deep meanings that never sleep

Rather they overleap the silence of sleep
Never bore us as you dance in your thesaurus
We become delirious discovering the mysterious
Like a dignitary inside your dictionary
Drinking from the distillery of the mystery
Hummingbirds feeding on your words

Your brilliance never asleep in the dictionary
A thesaurus of life delivers the mystery
So mysterious in all your words.

Navigating Deftly on Planet Earth, a sestina

Riding a deep breath, stops the pulsing heart,
enveloped in bed that whispers silence,
packed into the end of day, stars and moon.
The instant gravity keeps eyes open,
holds dreams at bay with centripetal force,
while America revolves in movement.

Natives of the Nile at night hear movement
on straw beds, goat-skin tents, inside the heart.
They taste Sahara winds and floods that force
them to count bleak days of ending silence,
time when the camel markets will open,
smell an oasis, orbit of the moon.

Sherpas at Mt. Everest touch the moon,
in stone houses they can grasp the movement,
abundance of stars, the sky is open.
With little oxygen around their hearts,
they see future memories and silence,
able to feel it all and grasp the force.

Tribes in the Amazon welcome the force
on floating villages under the moon,
bushmen hunting and fishing in silence,
anacondas weaving their own movement,
dire preservation taken to heart
while rainforests rotate to stay open.

All the rivers in Europe are open
markets along the banks sell to the force
of kings and queens, old armies of the heart,
centuries of wars, paintings of the moon.
The waters flow in the sea of movement
And history repeats in the silence.

Andromeda lights the Outback silence,
aboriginal songs wild and open,
a didgeridoo wails in the movement
of wild dingoes in herds driven by force,
silhouette of Uluru on the moon
portends untimely stillness to the heart.

Galactic movement, the world in silence,
interwoven beats the heart will open
and force the tides and shadows of the moon.

Till Death Do Us Partially, a prose poem

The drive to Salem Fields took a lifetime in the back seat of my
father's Buick Regal hearing the story of a con man who tried to
sell the Brooklyn Bridge suspended with steel cables between granite
towers. The span had more than taken its human toll of construc-
tion workers and those who jumped into the East River. An immi-
grant who entered through Ellis Island and lived a good life in both
boroughs, Isidor passed away naturally at ninety-six. I was in Santa
Rosa then, on my way to Argentina. Now we were driving from
Manhattan with my aunt to Salem Fields to visit him, say a prayer
in the mausoleum.

I was not able to be there for the funeral when he was dressed in the
suit that he wore every day, straightening the silverware on the dinner
table, and licking the salt from pretzels before returning them to the
bowl. His birthday was on Christmas Day, and every year he would
blow out the candles, and every year his wife would say, "Don't spit
on the cake, I.L." As a kid staying overnight in their apartment, we
watched the Friday night fights, bet a dollar and always won, slept on
the couch in the living room. He kept hard candies in his suit pocket
and read the evening paper sitting in his chair. He told me that every-
thing would be all right if I treated girls nicely.

We drove throughout the grounds without a map looking for the
gravesite, a rainy Saturday afternoon, the only car trying to find its
way. My father observed there was no one else around. His sister
echoed, "It's really dead around here." Memorials were everywhere
for husbands and wives, children and parents, some underground,
plots, caskets, crypts, and urns. Most everyone had new neighbors,
flowers fresh, wilted, and plastic. We eventually found our family
name carved on the grey granite building, had a key to open the
bronze door. All quiet now, one at a time, the building very small,
twelve crypts total, six on each side, eight above ground and four
below. The only occupants were above, Isidor, his brother Albert,
Albert's wife Bella and their son Jack. A drawer was saved for Jack's
wife Evy. I was destined for a room in the basement.

My father went in first and then my aunt. I was handed a small
prayer pamphlet, meditations from Riverside Memorial Chapel,
Hebrew on the right, transliteration on the left, Psalm 23 in English
in the valley of the shadow of death. I could pick kaddish to read
or say my own thing, which I chose. I never met Albert. Aunt Bella
always made me kiss her on the back of her neck, avoiding what
deadly disease I might have had.

The mausoleum had a smell of finality, musty like old age, stagnant. I said what I needed to say. The drive back was solemn, the traffic light. Private thoughts and silence were part of the ritual of dying, part of trying to find closure. When I saw my grandmother the next day, she observed that my side "whiskies" were long. She knew that I.L. was no longer around, her only comment, "That's the end of the story."

Three years later, she moved to the granite house, and I flew to the city for her funeral. She made the best doughnuts in the world every Sunday, kept her old wedding linen unopened in her closet, a Danish or two in her top dresser drawer. On one knee she would open her mini fridge, take out a kosher chicken from Barney Green-grass, kept a brown paper bag in a Maxwell House coffee tin, her wastebasket that she walked daily to the incinerator. Her morning coffee was half sugar and half milk, accompanied two fried eggs floating in butter. She never wanted her picture taken, covered her face with her feathered hat. She looked resolved, at peace in her open casket.

Years after Evy got her drawer, my parents were cremated, their ashes scattered above Enderby Cliffs overlooking the Okanagan Valley. The glaciers had retreated thousands of years ago, and now the snow was powder deep in sun. My wife and I rented a helicopter skiing at Silver Star, wore mittens, woolen hats, and thermal underwear, said a prayer, and released their ashes over the cliff. The wind blew them back into our faces, in our eyes.

The mausoleum needed perpetual care, but no one else was going there. The structure was half full and time was in another world, everyone had either moved on or moved out, passed on or passed away, started in one place and ended up in another. All the family secrets had been encrypted, the stories that have no end in sight were not over and had not been written.

I drive by cemeteries from time to time, have gone to funerals, been asked to say something, find words to celebrate, to help the living grieve. I see the tombstones along the side of the highway, mourners meandering and workers mowing the lawn. The mood is one of perpetual peace, respect for those who wish to make a visit and those who appreciate the company.

I canceled my subscription to Ancestry.com, planted all my family trees in a manilla folder. I search my soul, evaluate, and weigh myself every morning. Sometimes up and sometimes down, I never really know where I am going, but I can think more about that tomorrow morning.

The Gnome of Xi'an, a gnomic poem

Hidden in the basement of the Xi'an Hotel,
Buried as a terra cotta warrior
Destined to one job for life,
An overly loquacious travel agent
With red star pinned on his grey uniform
Desperately tried to arrange the journey
By train from the ancient capital to Chengdu,
The birthplace of five-star Sichuan cuisine.

In a milky green plastered room
With college English and crooked teeth,
Garlic tainting the frigid air
In the aftermath of twice cooked pork,
The extremely ambitious agent
Welcomed American companionship
And tried his communistic best to be sociable
Without a computer, cell phone, or WiFi,
To book an overnight expedition
And suitable hotel for a foreign expert's family
Of four and their young Chinese interpreter.

The agent and the expert spoke in English,
The latter interjecting what little Mandarin

He had learned in the past half year
From teaching bilingual college juniors,
The former interspersing proverbs from his classes
With exuberance and enthusiasm
That would enthrall Benjamin Franklin
And cause Confucius to turn over in his tomb.

Spring Festival was upon us, the Year of the Rat,
A sign of wealth, prosperity, and rapid reproduction
In a populous land of one family one child,
Wrapping dumplings and hanging red paper lanterns.
Travel a challenge with charges
Calculated on a wooden abacus,
The agent tried his best to be frugal,
Offering a ten-hour hard sleeper
Saying, "A penny saved is a penny earned."

We could hear premature, intermittent firecrackers,
Twelve million people
Unable to restrain their excitement,
Could imagine the famous restaurants
In Chengdu preparing their meals
And ordering cases of Mao Tai

At an intoxicating rate.
We needed to find a hotel,
A room that we could afford.
Assured by the agent that,
"All that glitters isn't gold,"
We would be near a famous pagoda
And could visit monkeys in the mountains.

With calligraphy on the walls,
Messages indecipherable, a pendant light bulb
Illuminated our attempts to interact.
We purchased bright red embroidered vests
From local peasants, climbed a hill
At the tomb of a Tang Dynasty emperor,
Commune members celebrating
The prosperity of tourism,
Embroidered snakes, toads,
Centipedes, scorpions, and spiders.
Confucius says, "Everything has its beauty,
But not everyone sees it."

The contemporary emperor in his catacomb,
Secluded and fixated,
Focused to book the impending excursion
Using words without definition.
Our need to travel as ambassadors
Of peace and friendship,
His goal to rise to a level higher above his cadre,
Very different worlds,
Like a convoluted lunar new year lion dance,
Came together in clasped hands

And smiles of good luck and fortune,
As he said with conviction,
"Actions speak louder than words."

Reflecting back, he did his level best
To welcome the new year,
A Chengdu banquet
Of multiple courses and drinking games,
Fireworks lighting up the Chongqing sky at midnight.
The Yangtze tide was out
Walking in the sand to the crowded ferry,
Navigating the three gorges,
Beacon lights marking depth levels,
Freezing in Wuhan, Guilin's Li River
Meandering through karst landscapes.
Confucius says, "It does not matter how slowly you go,
So long as you do not stop."

So now we have some silk and pieces of jade,
We have birds in our hands
And lead our horses to drink,
Going to bed and rising early,
Not judging books by their covers,
We remember a time out of sight
But not out of mind,
A time when common people
Enjoyed their common friendship.
We have our photos and memories
Categorized on a shelf.
Confucius says, "Do not do unto others
What you do not want done to yourself."

Crossing the Border in 1984, an epic poem

"BIG BROTHER IS WATCHING YOU." – George Orwell

Spring Festival in Beijing had just begun
The communists were packed and on the run
Traveling thousands of miles by hard sleeper
Trying to keep warm and out of harm.
Chongqing fireworks welcomed the new year
Like a world war
Three million people at midnight
Lighting one-inch crackers
Before daybreak our family of four
Ferrying down the Yangtze.
I showered one time
With water from the boiler room
A Foreign Expert talking naked
With a toothless peasant in Sichuanese
We both had two sons
On our way to freeze in Wuhan.

No one was free though they wanted to be
Socialist Ethics Month coming soon for the Party.
Karst landscapes in Guilin as we floated the Li
Goat hot pot for lunch Elephant Rock in view

Wife and boys flew to Hangzhou
To find West Lake covered in snow.
I got stuck at Guilin airport
One seat short to fly to Guangzhou
Needing to catch the ferry
To Hong Kong for an interview.
The baggage handler fluent in English
Offered to help with rules he had to follow
His only job assigned for life.

Everyone tried to beat the cadre
The convoluted web of leaders
Who met in the Great Hall of the People
Close to The Forbidden City.
Louis found one unoccupied seat
Two pilots stood and watched me eat
A fish caught that morning
Before I boarded the four-hour flight.
On the tarmac in Guangzhou
Dressed in Western attire two guys
Gave me a ride in their van
For ten yuan had to go fast
On the way needed to stop at Air China
To buy a ticket to Shanghai.

The office closed padlock on the door
Their best friend let me in
The flight sold out another friend
Found the last seat on the plane
In the van to the ferry dock
Everyone knew how to work the back door
Everyone had friends
Trying not to hit chickens in the street
Throngs of people crowding the wharf
Shouting for tickets to get on board
I raised my hand the only foreigner
The only one to get a deck seat.

Soldiers with rifles stopped me
At the end of the pier my visa unsigned
The ferry pulled out only six feet away
The crowd was gone no one around
Except a lone motorcyclist sped me to town.
The White Swan Hotel opulent
The walls pastel spectacular
Like the Temple of Heaven.
Needing the embassy early in the morning
I walked downtown ate chow mein
With students smoking Marlboros
Speaking English laughing drinking beer.

Breakfast dim sum the food kept coming
On carts a taxi to the consulate
My visa stamped to the train station
For a ticket on the express the doors locked

On the side of the building an open window
"Ni hao," a woman opened the door
No seats on the express only the local
And once again only one ticket
Three hours on a packed train.
Pulled into the station at Shenzhen
I did not know where to go
Looking at a half mile of tracks
Took my visa out of my slacks
The system confusing running out of luck
Friends and back doors
Wondered if I had to go through customs
I just walked across the border
Through a fence in plain view
Could not think of anything else to do
Left the PRC without a scene
And rode a subway to Sha Tin.

At the University of Hong Kong
Took a deep breath answered questions
Until they thanked me housed me in a dorm
The next morning found a room
At the YMCA walked around Kowloon
Leased to Great Britain for 99 years
The typhoon shelter by junk
Steered by a woman
Her child tethered to the mast.
Bought cheap suitcases and British toffee
Clorox and a can of Yuban coffee
The night market everyone shopping

With Hong Kong dollars
Eating octopus and squid lots of tentacles
At tables with bottles of VSOP
Food carts of all sorts filled every street
Serving skewers of grilled chicken feet.

In the morning on time for the express
To Guangzhou and then to the airport
Ticket in hand at the gate "*Fēijī wèi dàole*"
Fogg canceled the flight.
Returned to the Swan dialed information
Connected right away to my wife
At the Park Hotel on Nanjing Road
They knew where all the foreigners were staying
Kept track of western bourgeois decadence
The next morning my flight was quick
Toured the harbor jade and ivory factories
Until the train to Beijing
Played chess talked stamps bought meals
When I opened my wallet to pay
A wall of people looked inside
Wondered about the value of my Visa card.

I had crossed the forbidden border
Crossed back three days outside the PRC
Over my shoulder Chairman Mao was watching me
Embalmed in his Memorial Hall
His final resting place in a glass case
Open to the public with the people
Standing in line watching him

Looking revolutionary pale and grave.
The holiday over did not get the job
Returned to teach English on the mainland
With a comrade hired to tap my phone
And read my mail now I knew the rules
That everyone apparently tried to break.
People told to stand in line
Had never seen a big nose
A child's blue eyes blond hair,
People who wanted to breathe fresh air
Only five years before Tiananmen Square.

Haidian Market, free verse

Breathe in a peculiar freedom
Driving a one-speed Phoenix bicycle
Through the streets of northwest Beijing
Throngs of turbulent shoppers
Woven bags of cabbages
Mandarin oranges bananas and melons

I have no bank account
No checkbook
Keep my *renminbi* in a desk drawer
In the living room
Where the *fuwuyuan* cleans the floor
With an oily mop
Moves the dead cockroaches
Across the terrazzo
From apartment to apartment

I could tell our phones were tapped
Could hear the breathing
Could smell the garlic
I had a portable typewriter
And sent letters to the states
Like the mail we received that was opened

Nothing regular mattered in this communist freedom
Where workers dug up streets one day
Returned them to normal the next
And excavated again the following day by hand

My broken bicycle wobbled from stall to stall
Ringing its bell then paused
Bought some fruit and vegetables
Found a repair shop
And got pounded with a wrench
Everything back to working well
With a little oil and a cordial smile

The moon at night looked the same
As the common people shared their food
While the leaders followed rules
The rice spoke Chinese
And the beer was warm and familiar

The Greystone Hotel, couplets

Apartment 216 was down the hall
The smell of kosher chickens wall to wall
On Broadway people sat on benches in the island
Between the traffic flowing both directions
Above noisy subway grates sat friends and strangers
Isidore always wore a tie with his suit
Betty's hat covered with artificial fruit
Her homemade doughnuts a weekly treat
The Hole in the Wall deli across the street
Served corned beef, tongue, and hot pastrami
After Sunday School, sandwiches for lunch
At the card table watching *The Lone Ranger* ride again
Into those thrilling days of yesteryear
On the Upper West Side an island on an island
Where growing up took every day in stride
And looking back it all feels just the same
An era that can always be reclaimed
Whenever the mood strikes
And takes the time to live forever

Dear Ms. Lovejoy Muchmore, an epistolary poem

It seems like only yesterday I wrote to you.
Where the time has gone, I have no idea.
I have not yet received reply,
And thus, I fret that you have passed me by.

My letter last was lengthy and obtuse,
I beat around the bush, much too vague.
I should have better expressed my mind
And not left feelings undefined.

Yes, you have captured my every thought.
I waste no time now to let you know
That I have dreamed of you every single day
Since that first time we drank some Beaujolais.

Or maybe it was cabernet or pinot noir,
A merlot or a full-bodied Syrah.
Though my exact memory might be misled,
I am pretty sure that it was red.

I cherish a crystal-clear vision of you,
Whether or not your hair was blonde or brunette.
What mattered most from the very start
Were the ardent feelings burning in my heart.

I hope that your heart felt the same,
Quivered with delight as we toasted
On that special occasion I am concentrating,
Though I cannot remember exactly what we were celebrating.

Perhaps that first encounter or our future union,
Years of joyously living our lives together.
Please do not take me for a dunce,
Even though we have only met once.

I would readily get down on my knee,
Though in a letter I would have to draw a picture,
I confess that I am not the smartest,
I am also not very much of an artist.

However, I believe I know why you have not written,
Because I am the only one who is smitten.
The thoughts I share with you are too pedantic,
A far cry from anything romantic.

So, take this letter and rip it into shreds.
Go to sleep, do not forget your meds.
I know that you just need a little space
And that this letter deserves the fireplace.

This is my final goodbye, adieu, so long,
I wish that I could turn it into a song,
A tune of unrequited love so fervent,
As I remain sincerely your humble servant.

Growing Old is for the Aged, a double acrostic

Gardens prune themselves until they are dead,
rows of once yellow dandelions, a withering sight to see,
own the vacant estate in all their fuzziness, blowing
windward to start their next life in a freshly planted era.
Inert gardeners with rusty steel shovels, indistinguishable,
nod themselves to a restless sleep within a sepia photograph,
gentle yet inspired by reoccurring dreams of disillusionment.
Old, faded memories that will not last forever,
lying one on top of the other, like an eroded archipelago,
distant from the barren land and barely weatherproof,
ignore in slumber the subtle changes of the seasons.

Villain *L*, a villanelle

Will someone pray for Villain *L*
And the other twenty-five,
Giving life in man-made hell?

Only words could possibly tell
The messages we derive.
Will someone pray for Villain *L?*

Buried in tomes and forced to yell,
Phrases attempt to connive,
Giving life in man-made hell.

Clauses crawling from their cell,
Cunning images contrive.
Will someone pray for Villain *L?*

A letter waiting for a spell
From those who barely seem alive,
Giving life in man-made hell.

Their speeches never meaning well,
Poison pens will not survive.
Will someone pray for Villain *L,*
Giving life in man-made hell?

Emotions in Motion, cinquains

Below,
So very deep,
Will not appear to show,
Cannot be seen or heard to weep,
Asleep.

Above,
So very high,
A flight to fall in love
And soar with the wind in front of
The sky.

Within,
Hold back all doubt,
Trust all that you can see,
Truth will out, cannot live or be
Without.

Broken Wing, haiku

Fallen from the tree,
I try to lift my head, but
cannot see the sky.

The Milky Way: Gas, Dust, and Gravity, diamantes

i.

Day
Light Active
Waking rising working
Sunrise dawn dusk sunset
Resting sleeping dreaming
Dark passive
Night

ii.

Sun
Yellow spherical
Providing heating sustaining
Life warmth navigation constellation
Sparkling shining shooting
Luminous celestial
Star

Welcome to the Broadmoor, a pantoum

We share a room at our destination
in time to make our reservation
you only live once
in our salvation

In time to make our reservation
we unpacked the baggage
in our salvation
acting without hesitation

We unpacked the baggage
from some preparation
acting without hesitation
our hearts beating in unison

From some preparation
we played tennis in the sun
our hearts beating in unison
as we fell into love

We played tennis in the sun
baked Alaska for dessert
as we fell into love
and laughed with our hearts

Together at last and forever
we share a room at our destination
decide to stay another night
you only live once

Away from the Snow and Into the Desert, an alphabet poem

Alaska Airlines premium class, River calm in carrier under the seat,
Buick Encore reserved at Thrifty, Palm Springs Airport,
California warmth and sunshine, arrived on time,
   baggage claimed, and ready to
Drive in the desert to a rental destination with an
Expired driver's license, a stop at Stater's for bottled water, but then
Frustrated with horrid condo, conditions not as advertised.

Got out of there immediately, left the mess,
   and found a pet-friendly place,
Hyatt Regency Resort and Spa, king room with bathrobes,
Indian Wells nestled in the Coachella Valley,
Joshua Tree boulders nearby in the Upper Mojave, ocotillo,
   cholla, agave sunset,
Ketchup in mini bottles, Heinz 57 and Worcestershire for the grill,
Leafy greens, Mexican zucchini, cherub tomatoes and vinaigrette.
Mango is ripe, avocados feel ready, a million grapefruits with
Nonchalance among bottles of Topo Chico and
Oranges chilling in the mini fridge.
Plunge in the jetted spa at will and be
Quiet and peaceful, refreshed and rejuvenated,
Resting and relaxing even though the
Seahawks lost to the Packers by five.

Taking River for walks every morning, riding a recumbent bike
   at Aqua Serena Spa
Ubiquitous sunshine enveloping the fully refunded
VRBO vacated to a Villa vacation, a vegan lunch
   at the Natural Sisters Cafe
Warm curried rice wrap and avocado black bean burger
Xanthous sun while luxury camping, grilling on the barbecue
Yucca palms tell fortunes a day at a time while
Zzz emojis bid tonight sleep tight and rise and shine tomorrow.

Escape to Old San Juan, dos *Puerto Rican décimas*

i.

The red-eye flight from JFK
Landed softly, all applauded
Tourist bars in town, marauded
Bacardi poured a getaway
Coconuts ice cold paved the way
To Luquillo Beach in the sun
Hordes of *amigos* having fun
My Honda 50 out of gas
Drunk sailors sang at Midnight Mass
Until the new year had begun

ii.

Ten-foot waves at Arecibo
A lobster boiled in a can
On the beach, looking very tan
I might climb a hill tomorrow
I barely know where I will go
Eat some *pan*, whatever I bring
The Caribbean Sea will sing
At Mayaguez to replenish
As I try to speak in Spanish
Understanding everything

Two Moons Orbiting the Earth, a *lục bát*

Hong cuts hair at Great Clips,
Her scissors transform snips to styles,
She greets me with warm smiles.
Her home in Saigon miles away,
Takes the day off Tuesday,
Goes shopping anyway for fruits,
One of her attributes caring
For Mom at home, sharing their meals,
Cooking pho that appeals.
Sends me coupons and deals each year,
Trims just above the ear,
She's happy to be here at work,
Always laughs not a smirk.
She often finds a perk for me,
Nine haircuts, the tenth free.
She likes to eat bánh mì for lunch,
And some challah to munch
Before she starts to scrunch my hair,
Tell stories that we share.
Humor without a care runs on,
Much joy in the salon,
Until the fun is gone for now,
We're good friends anyhow.

Will still remain so when I leave,
Senior discounts receive,
We will always believe in us.
English words we discuss,
Pronounce them with no fuss, like kin,
Our relationship a win Nguyen.
Where we end, we begin,
We know ourselves within our world.
My hair is always curled,
The barber cape is furled carefree,
We celebrate with glee,
Lunar new year sticky rice cake,
This memory is our keepsake.
I say goodbye and ache with her,
Our decade was a blur
That passed like a solar eclipse.

III

A Dance Horizontal

Floradora Meets Dora and the Dreadful Dragon

The Honored Queen spoke French
As she carved her way around the moguls.
On ungroomed mountain trails,
Floradora one of her favorites,
Her curly hair tucked into her purple ski hat,
Her lips glistening with Estee Lauder cream.
All the moguls in Aspen turned their heads downhill
To ogle at the alpine fox gliding black diamond terrain
In the panorama of majestic Maroon Bells,
Overlooking the winding Roaring Fork
On her way to the barn on McLain Flats Road.
Norwegian cross-country skiers at Ashcroft
Toasted her arrival with a raucous "*skoal*,"
Cheered her at the Paragon, the Hotel Jerome,
And the rustic Woody Creek Tavern.

Duke David had a darling daughter named Dora
And lived on Sesame Street in a child's book.
The single father of a three-year old son
Carried this story wherever they went,
From the Montessori school to Cinderella City,
Driving together in a Corolla SR-5,
Cooking gourmet meals and doing daily laundry.

A shepherd cross named Basil along for the ride,
Wooden skies stored in the closet
With tie-up boots and a woolen hat.
Life was finally grand in Arvada,
A condo for a castle with very little hassle.

Neither ever wanted to marry again,
Never be a bride or groom,
Even though something invisible was wanting,
A longing like a sensual vapor.
Until the night they met by chance,
That very first glance like the diamond D
Duke David hung around Dora's dimpled neck.
Everyone else worried about the Dreadful Dragon of Dundeedle
While they talked about Campari and Crème de Cassis
Had no worries and lost their fears
Uncontrollably indulging themselves in romance
As they read the story to the son and laughed page after page
While Dora thought that the dragon was a doggie,
And Basil slept peacefully on the floor.

First Seder

Temple Emanuel Judaica shop on Grape Street
Had a paperback Haggadah
And a blue, white, and gold seder plate
With a place for the shank bone
In both Hebrew and English.
Every King Soopers in Denver
Carried Manischewitz Concord Grape,
Gefilte fish in liquid broth, matzoh of affliction
Horseradish of tradition, and coconut macaroons.
My most recent plagues were seemingly over,
And I was romantically inspired to roast a brisket,
Make charoset, chicken soup, and potato kugel.
What could be more enchanting in courtship,
More sensually Kosher for Passover,
Than an ancient meal to celebrate emancipation?

Driving three hours over Independence Pass to Aspen
To share this freedom in love with my lady,
Paschal prayers, a banquet, and spiritually sweet wine,
Taking turns reading from right to left,
Drinking way more than four Kiddush cups
Of the fruit of the vine,
United our liberated spirits
In a modern culinary worship service,

Light as fluffy matzoh balls floating to the surface,
Joyously experiencing the transformation
From being alone to being together.

This night was different from all other nights,
This festival of our internal lights,
Illuminated by candles and the radiant glow
Only experienced by the hearts of lovers
Who have had their share of bitter herbs,
Have dipped parsley into their salty tears,
Now free from former burdens,
Having bathed their bodies and souls in wine
And discovered new life,
A soothing voice.
Rejoice! Rejoice! Rejoice!
It would have been enough. *Dayenu!*

The Life of My Love

We have reached the point of all returns,
Moments in a world of our own,
The universe with its concerns,
A cosmos that we have known
Still exists in some reality,
Yet our new place is timeless and totally free.

We are outside the realm of distant lands,
Living each day in front of the other,
Exploring ourselves and holding hands,
Stacking each minute on top of another,
We do our thing in random stages,
Like an open book turning its own pages.

I do not know how I could live without you,
How to navigate each day and night.
I would be lost and fall through
The loneliness that presents itself with every daylight,
But for now we rise and watch the incoming weather
That comes along as we live our lives together.

Marriage

A young woman walks to the edge of Puget Sound,
To the rugged shore where a flurry of majestic waves
Lap the sandy caves
Of hermit crabs buried under the rocks
Among seaweed, kelp,
And sculptures of ancient driftwood.

With arms outstretched above the silhouettes of salmon fishermen
Drifting leeward off the beach at Spee-bi-dah,
She looks solemnly into the swirling sky,
And with a voice dainty yet determined,
Asks the question, "What is marriage?"

As the cumulonimbi disperse
And the sky takes on the hue of the setting sun,
The answer fills her palpitating heart.

It is all those romantic movies,
Those 19th century romance novels,
Candlelight, red wine, crooning love songs.
Sibelius, being swept off your feet,
Held in his arms, a knight in shining armor,
A poet, a lover, a *mensch*,
Commitment, no guarantees, security, partnership,
When two become one.

It is Aspen Airways commuter tickets, vows under the *chuppah*,
Flannel nightgowns, sharp toenails, snoring,
Breathe-rite strips, snowing, skiing,
Seafood restaurants, flights to France, grilled salmon,
Baked halibut, becoming old in rocking chairs together,
Hormones and whispers, a toaster oven,
Someone to pay the Nordstrom bill, balance the checkbook,
Change your oil, *Erotic Art of the East*, taking out the garbage,
Serving you coffee in the morning, giving you a baby,
Taking you where no one has ever taken you before,
Completely satisfied, living in bliss,
Living in happiness, a kiss that lingers on the lips,
Living happily ever after.

A young man waxes a pair of cross-country skis
And trudges upwards to the top of a snowy mountain,
To the blistery apex where the air is nonexistent
And the sky has joined the universe.
With his eyes frozen solid and his lips stuck together,
He manages to breathe the burning question,
"What is marriage?"

The answer comes to him in the faint headlights
Of the snow cats Grooming Aspen Mountain,
The frost illuminated by a miner's lamp,
And the festive song of drunken Norwegians.

It is the laughter of a sweet voice at your side,
A welcome long-distance phone call,
Curly hair brushing across your cheek, a sleeping beauty,
The love songs of Mary McCaslin, a soul mate,
A Jewish American princess dressed in a see-through *schmata*,
An eternal companion, Vulpecula, the pounding in your heart,
An untouched chocolate heart for Valentine's Day,
Your best friend, homemade coleslaw, the perfumed air,
The lip cream, the delicate touch, the silk nails,
Chinese restaurants, watching golf on television, bagels and lox,
Cel-Ray tonic, someone who makes the bed a special way,
Arranges fresh flowers, sings in the morning, living in bliss,
A kiss that lingers on the lips,
Living happily ever after.

The young woman and the young man got married,
And got remarried a quarter of a century later
Under a *chuppah* in a Persian restaurant.
Once again, in a new time that seemed
Both a moment and an eternity,
Their eyes searched their hearts,
Their hearts searched their souls,
Their hands would have searched their loins had they not been in public,
And their minds and bodies became entwined
In a realm that was both known and unknown,
Old and new, clear yet idyllic.

Once again, the world stopped moving
As they repeated their vows,
And a brand new reality rekindled emotions
That had been strengthened by time.
This was love, the meaning of life.
This was marriage, this was bliss, and this was the way,
The only way, that it was meant to be, forever after.

The Liquor on Her Lips

I often see a smile reserved
For certain private times
Intimate moments illuminated
By her hazel eyes

French kissing in the morning
An everlasting emblem of love
Especially if one partner is fluent
And the other got a "D" in high school

When her eyes are closed
I can imagine where she might be
Somewhere inside of me
Spread open embracing my heart

Hearing the phrase, "I love her to death"
And the bouquet of her breath
As I can read her mind
Finish her sentences

I step out of the shower
Singing Peter, Paul, and Mary
Where have all the towels gone
Lying in bed naked

She tastes like warm snow
An impossible fragrance
That rolls around my tongue
Asking for indulgence

Flesh on flesh
Wrapped in arms and legs
Lips that speak in silence
Touching each other like best friends

She shines the most inside
Quenches every thirst
With a luscious melody that I can follow
Entwined together until the final swallow

No Guarantees

Some things you can take back
Say just kidding, psych,
Didn't mean it.
Some are as permanent
As permanent can be
Like superglue on your fingers
Dental implants that change your smile.

When it comes to ardent love
That's another story.
Commitments like marriage
Spiral as smoke forms
Underneath a fire cloud
Of returns, reconciliation, and divorce
That once walked down the aisle.

Every form asks for marital status.
How do you fit that in a single box?
Like trying to answer the sex question
With either male or female.
It's a lot more complicated than that,
Like bearing children
And having an argument every once in a while.

Some love is soothing
Like effleurage at the right time,
Always carries pleasantries and risks,
Welcome gifts, good nights, and good mornings,
Little moves that remind you
Of what is really real,
Eternal and not on trial.

Years

Life changed years ago today
And every day thereafter.
True to the core and true tomorrow,
Our breath blows the breeze
And holds hands at daylight,
Withstanding changes that were more dramatic than others.
Some more like idylls, others like thunder;
None as predictable as tides,
Shooting stars, and a variety of snowflakes.

We are moving in space now,
Whispers in the galaxy.
The rain like perspiration,
Droplets wiped away with the back of a hand,
Wash away each gesture
And uncover the latest budding thought.

Time has not changed anything
Other than the rings of trees
And the overgrowth of secret forests.
We are amazed that we are amazed,
Gathered in our own fragile cloth,
Distinguished by a few chosen words,
And celebrating as many moments as we possibly can.

Invitation to Your Anniversary

Dress is casual
obligatory but not mandatory
figure out the year
and find a gem

RSVP hopefully
I'll be there
if you wish
rack of lamb
would be a good dish

to serve for just
the two of us
soften the lights
enjoy the meal

one of a million
in many ways
over many days
and especially this one

How Long Do I Have to Wait for My Champagne?

Chilling in the fridge
For over a decade
And moved from shelf to shelf
Rotated over different memories
And bidding farewell
To boundless meals
Pinot Gris and bottled water

The timing is not always right
But when the cork orbits the sun
It won't be flat
As each bubble will tell a story
But for now I look at it every day
As it whispers to me with potential effervescence
An always constant presence

A celebration stops the action
While the action is a celebration in itself
Wondering what to do next
Where to go
Like a drop of water
Waiting to be dropped
Condensation holding hands
With evaporation

Anticipation is the taste of excitement
On the palate
Of one who does not mind the wait
One who waits in reverie
On the doorstep of revelry
At the threshold of eternity

Still the Words Now

Lower the shades and pull back the covers
Clear the mind of activity and ritual
The lovers fed their pets as usual
And tended to mundane routines not spiritual.

What was once a day of lists and tasks
Dissolves into a meld of shadows.
The masks are off and on the pillows,
Leaving behind what might have mattered.

The mattress rotates eastward around its axis
As lights go off and stars go on.
The ashes tell a story of contentment
Tasked to lie in sleepy stillness.

The memory recounts the day before
Prepares to empty into dream.
Recumbent thoughts not what they seem
Slide into bed together in their arms.

Some last words bond their union
And get comfortable in repose.
Relax their muscles begin to dose
And travel in peace with their souls.

What could be more perfect than to take a sleep
Napping side by side in harmony
Creating shallow breaths and memory
With eyes closed until tomorrow.

Talking in Her Sleep

She said that she's more tired
in the morning than when she went to sleep.
"Ok, so you have to put what the building location is and mark it private."
Exhausting dreams remembered as they keep coming back,
failing exams, arriving late to class,
unable to find the right room, missing assignments.
She said, *"My car got stolen again,"*
but I was busy deep-sea diving.
"We'll find another way. We'll just change something."

Waking up to realize the dream,
recounting people and repeated places, blended together.
"Ok. Find out. River's not from Colorado."
Phrases mumbled softly in French.
"Oui, la nuit porte conseil."
Teaching students to learn how to learn.
"I was hired to start the ESL program, um, hmm.
Yes, they're professional teachers. They teach. I do know the students.
Sign. S-s-s-i-n-e. We're not spelling the word. What do you hear? The g is silent."

Words that could have meaning,
expressions of caring and hope.
I'm just very grateful that he's doing so well."
Time and space all out of place.
"You think she'll go in eighty years? Um, hmm.
Ok, oh good."
Awake several times in the night
and relatively awake in the morning.

She said she had the craziest dream.
"Is it stormy outside?" Did you hear something?"
Thunder, an airplane, a bear knocking over the garbage,
the furnace, a bird flying into the window
all possibilities.
Exhausted, she retells in graphic detail
a crazy convoluted story of comedy and tragedy,
laughing and screaming,
put to rest in the recollection,
stirred with a cup of coffee
and a tepid shower that washes away adventure
and sets the scene for what she'll see tonight
when the circadian rhythm moves into the bedroom
and turns on the music.

The Blinds Were Nice in the Middle of the Night

Outside wild animals overtook the country
Cities were armed with viral strains
And time was running out of energy
As we hid insular tucked in our beds
Turning over to adjust
Whatever machines we were hooked up to
Trying to save our lives
Or at least live a little longer
As some started to use the word *Armageddon*
While remaining anonymous
Behind scriptures
Incognito around everything they could not understand

We were taught not to use the word *stupid*
So of course we used it
Every chance we had
Which was pretty much all the time
When we were around stupid people
Who said stupid things
When they were out of control during the day
And dreamed stupid dreams
During the night when they tossed and turned
And should have fallen off the edge of this flat earth

So we have a choice among shutters shades and blinds
Nuclear radiation shields
And sleeping under lead blankets
Anything to block out the deafening sounds of chaos
Police sirens and military helicopters
That drop bombs and pamphlets
Advertising diet pills miracle drugs and imitation bacon
Thumb drive bibles and instant pregnancy tests
To save the planet and stop the noise

Blinds were a good choice
Between sunset and sunrise
Like leather blinders on a dappled horse
Only looking forward and staying on track
Nothing will spook us on our pillows
As we stare straight ahead at the ceiling
And deny that we have insomnia
Only a bad case of worrywarts
In the end stage of anxiety
But treatable

Wake Up Call

Lying in bed trying not to move
Controlling every breath
And feeling the rotation of the earth
Around its axis
I can't wait until you wake up

Memories are like meteors
Tangled in the sheets
Conspiring to shift darkness into daylight
As you breathe into the pillows
Of dreams from distant galaxies

I'm ready to plan the day
Create a calendar balance the checkbook
Take something out of the freezer for dinner
Pull up the shades
And see what weather has in store

I would like to touch your arm
Knowing that you are alive
But wary to disturb your sleep
To interrupt the woven universe
That slumbers in the linen

The phones are all turned off
The lights are out
The day has really not begun
And yet I can hear the wind outside
And the stillness on the inside

I try to blink loud enough for you to hear
A subtle announcement that I cannot live this life alone
Maybe the sprinklers will turn on and wake you up
The dog will roll over and the cat will jump on the bed
And I will pretend to be asleep as you wait until I wake up

Let the Candles Extinguish by Themselves

Each day becomes a candle at night
the wax drips down a wine bottle
a romantic stalactite flowing
over itself onto a glass plate until exhausted

The flame writes notes in the air
illuminates the still moments
the faint times of love and loss
when hearts seek some glimmer of light

Tonight it feels soft and warm
until tomorrow brittle and fragile
words having touched each other in the flickering light
wake up to something more blindingly bright

With her head on his shoulder she shared her thoughts
he remembered everything that he should have told her
their lives burned gently together flowing away
as the next candle listened to what they had to say

Love Letters

There are two shoeboxes in the closet,
like winter clothes in summer,
several years of romance
enveloped in postal delivery
and mailed from one place to another.
Some of the letters are still alive,
permanently stamped in memories,
priority mail that requires no postage
or even a return address.

We take the boxes with us wherever we go
just in case the weather changes,
sometimes reading a few
and wondering who wrote what,
sometimes writing a new letter
or a note for a special occasion,
a poem here or there
accompanied by a photo,
no flowers or jewelry.

Now we need to toss some of the letters,
having served their purpose or no purpose at all,
not meaningful to anyone but ourselves.
When someone else opens the box,

will it be empty or full of daring expressions,
lust and promises that have been kept,
amorous encounters and delicious moments
that end in a box for eternity.

Making the Bed

Take me to bed
The day is over or just beginning
Rituals are winding down
And somewhere between hospital corners
And oversized pillows
The past is wrapped
In the arms of Morpheus

Sometimes the bed is rumpled
Disgruntled like a child
Sulking in the corner
Mischievous and yet inviting
Slide into me
And make yourself at home

Other times taut and rigid
Can bounce a quarter off the sheets
An ordeal to crawl into
Impossible to turn over
Impaled by the Marquis de Sade
Gripping the neck and ankles

Someone usually sets the stage
Picks the hour to reset and recharge
When they look into each other's eyes
And realize they are in sleepy unison
But when it comes to making the bed
They can leave the covers in disarray
Because not everything can be determined
And some beds need to be made another day

Ylang-ylang

The art of buying perfume
Rubbing oil on the back of your wrist
And imagining what she would smell like
Lying in bed naked
As you take off your clothes
Remains a mystery
Hidden deep in tropical forests

Where you must pick the flowers
At just the right time
And touch her neck gently
With tremoring lips
Deft fingers caressing the nape
While you hum a tune
The notes an aphrodisiac

The price you pay inconsequential
The moment circumstantial
Writhing from a distant land
And wrapped the sweetest way
In an aroma that transforms fantasy
Into arms and legs
Bodies coming together
And breathing themselves over and over

Crash Landing on You and Others

We watch Korean romantic comedies
On Netflix with subtitles
From Seoul to Jeju Island,
Young men and women in their twenties and thirties
Eating spicy *ramyeon* and drinking *soju*,
Resorting to hangover soup
When their instant pre-packaged relationships get difficult to swallow,
Like dried vegetables and artificial flavoring,
Pollock, anchovies, and seaweed.

We definitely understand *Hanguk-eo*,
Turn up the volume to feel it vibrate,
Watch her cry and him try to console,
Walking on a vibrant running path
By the Han River, almost holding hands,
But tentative and cautious for five or more episodes,
Unable to say "like" and "love" and eventually kiss.

The past is cast with parents and grandparents
Working hard at making kimchi,
Favorite side dishes to store in the fridge,
Memories of hardship, deaths in the family,
Funeral customs and columbaria,
Failing shops with fewer customers,
In the park or at the beach,
Once crowded buses empty going home late
With tears, loneliness, and desperation.

Finally they hold hands and look into their eyes,
Laugh together over *bulgogi,*
Japchae, and *tteokbokki,*
Feed each other small pieces
Of grilled meat and remind us
Of when we were hungry
And ate at all hours of the night.

Our living room is decorated like South Korea,
And the house smells like fried chicken.
We are the actors in each series,
Translated into English,
Once as young as they are today,
Following an identical script in our own way.

Down to Earth at the Guemes Island Resort

The tide is coming in
hailed by a gallery
of driftwood, broken shells
and a shrill bird or two.

A lone oil tanker
waits between the islands
a gray whale out of place
spouting plumes of dark smoke.

The port not far away
complete with other ships
those much more fortunate
than the one held at sea.

Maybe there will never
be a free slip for her
to turn off her engines
secure in the harbor.

Maybe there will only
be more days at anchor
never free like us, watching as
the tide goes out.

Alternate Line Poems by Husband, Wife, and Two Sons

The Tower, by Sean

Start with a theme then a structure direction for what will follow
From the tower through the lens the population under siege
Writhes in shrouds of multicolored cloths
And yet we wear of which they sew
Constrained by stricture and directed to grow
In an endless evolving charade
Then the people tried to take control and spoke of peace
Words on the ground like frozen leaves that crack beneath the soldier's feet
Shards of broken glass reflect like shattered dreams
Far across the sea this seems the re-education camp's decree
Continue with a thought then the heart follows with introspection
Ask yourself the way in which this time a past reflection
Of stars that shine bright into the wind of peace and prevalence
Birthing truth into this new era upon us
Hello parent and baby can we guide you to the circus
It's the greatest show on the edge of earth
Precariously near the end of this journey together clasping hands
Will we remain a part of this world or relinquish our claim on the land
Will we disappear into the galaxies as unremarkable dust
Or take the time to recognize that those across the sea are us

Stars, by Aaron

Start with a theme then a structure direction for what will follow
Stars shine bright as a leading position even with imposition
In a dream fractured hollow and robotic
People in today's society live as chaotic protagonists
Skewed with little knowledge misguided they make mistakes
Who will heed our forefathers and rise up and lead our nation
The deceived and deluded tormented and confused argue with each other
And absurdly all the world's leaders ponder this same contemplation
Despair and destruction run rampant with no resolve apparent
Like children without guidance toddlers throwing temper tantrums
Continue with a thought then the heart follow with introspection
Into peace and prevalence to drown the blinding force
And stay the course through lows to highs into unconditional memories
Potbellied demigods squander away the roots and core values
This great nation is founded on and chide us as expendable
On a ledge the population under siege by a revolving relentless charade
Of varied precepts and perceptions sold to them a twisted agenda
Throwing contradictory into the wind
Our nation's values at the expense of the masses
A means to an end by those in power they write their own rules
Mocking the ones they fight against making no sense why they feud
Over all topics that matter but mainly to them
A debacle not transparent only has room for disaster
So right the wrongs and sing new songs
Don't settle for easy and sit idle while the world collapses
For time goes on and journeys are traveled
With some believing that patriotism is the glue
That holds the common of the greater good together

Unconditional Love, by Roberta

Start with a theme, then a structure, direction for what will follow
High Holy Days, Guide for the Jewish Homemaker, beloved recipes
And prayers that nourish body, soul, and spirit.
Bagel Nosh, lox and whitefish, "Are you Jewish?"
He laughed, shared smoked sable; she phoned next morning,
"Are you for real?" "Hello, Lady," Sean, Ringling Bros.
Barnum & Bailey Circus, Basil, Tory in Arvada,
Cotton candy, early days of the greatest show on earth.
Egg foo young for breakfast? Single parent, gourmet chef? Hmmm.
No guarantees, growing old in rocking chairs together,
I want to give you a baby, chuppah, Aaron, dissertation, Dr. Schmearput.
Continue with a thought, then the heart, follow with introspection,
"Do you want to go to China?"
Far across the sea, this seems the way, this time, a new era upon us
Wàiguórén, Youyi Binguan, Beijing, Xi'an, Chengdu, Chongqing...
Rise up and ponder this, chaotic masses, core values,
And topics apparent like children, eighteen years on MI, our first home,
Parenting and working through lows to highs.
The bond has no end in sight, the journey a knot that's tied and tight,
Two more homes, memories of travel, a boat, Winnie, River, and retire,
Two Stressless recliners, more modern than rockers,
United in accordance with the rite of Israel,
One family, unconditional love, what's to come? *L'Chaim!*

[Structure: These poems were written separately, a line at a time, by
four people. Ken wrote the first line; Sean, Aaron, and Roberta each
wrote a second line, Ken wrote the third line, and so on. The first and
the eleventh or twelfth lines are the same in all three poems. All the

poems contain the word "end" near the end of the poem. *The Tower* has words/phrases from *Stars* and *Unconditional Love* in the second half of the poem, *Stars* has words/phrases from *The Tower* and *Unconditional Love* in the second half, and *Unconditional Love* similarly has words/phrases from *The Tower* and *Stars*. Aside from Ken, no one saw the other poems until they were all finished.]

Cloistered in the Sonoran Desert 2020

Barrel cacti flower in the dusty sun
    bougainvillea spread their magenta bracts at noon
    roadrunners run cuckoo across the empty valley
    as COVID-19 has forced time to stand by itself alone

You can breathe no sense in the contrast between Netflix and news
    with racism an out-of-control pandemic in itself
    as masked protestors vacillate between anger and hope
    people trying to breathe with a knee to their throat

We exhale suspended yet privileged in a bubble
    squeezing juice from Cara Cara oranges,
    while the rest of the world inhales with pain
    and beats its head against walls of injustice

Fragile and fatigued in the chasm between wealth and poverty
    a valley of deserted souls needing to be rescued,
    with the privileged isolated from discord and destruction
    and the impoverished quarantined from opulence and opportunity

We exist in time drawn in the heat of the desert sun
    full of life and lifeless all the same
    disconnected at home from a surreal kind of reality
    yet hopeful despite all else in a new reality that has no name

Reflections at 4:00 AM on my 73rd Birthday

I bought our first tank of gas yesterday
in more than a month
just don't drive around much
now that we're in the desert
locked down with COVID-19
and ordered to stay at home
use our re-furbished golf cart
to get to the driving range
putting course and pool
at this last resort

This doesn't feel very much like a desert
somewhere in time
between Thanksgiving, Chanukah, Christmas, and New Year's
suddenly I am not able to access the internet
my network can't be found my memory pressure is high
and all my applications will be closed
but I will make chicken soup today anyway
put it in the fridge to render off the fat
make matzoh balls on Thursday
pray for Kosher wine and light the first candle

My wife woke up and asked what I am doing
I said that I am trying to get on the internet
she wished me a happy birthday
ate a bowl of shredded wheat
and went back to sleep
I restarted my computer
and was able to get on Safari
somewhere in the desert
accessible ordered and driven
a year older and wide awake

Another Day in Paradise with My Gardener

My husband does the grocery shopping
And most of the cooking
He grills the steaks and salmon
Brisket for the Jewish holidays
Chicken soup when we have colds
Picks Meyer lemons from our desert tree
Satisfies me in every way

He tends to the flower beds
The hummingbirds and the bees that buzz
He's also really good in bed or was
We never really had a date night
Never really needed one
Without jumping up and down
We figured out how to create fun

When I didn't want jewelry he gave me some
A flower when I didn't ask for one
He knows how to work the remote control
Gets the mail and does his own laundry
Takes out the garbage every Sunday
Scores a ten on my opinion poll

Our life is not a Hallmark card
Though this somewhat rhyming poem sounds like one
I hope he doesn't put it in his book
As it's just a bunch of gobbledygook
Though I really do love our garden of eating
This idyllic state that bears repeating
That my husband is very cultivated and clever
And that he never finds fault with all my bleating

Folding My Wife's Laundry

Warm cotton fabric smells of fragrant lavender,
Fresh out of the dryer soft and pleasing,
As free as a cloud on a lazy day,
And as personal as unscented body lotion.
Doll pants and tiny socks get folded,
Carefully put in a drawer,
Side by side with blouses and lingerie,
The act a private ceremony,
Like touching skin, fingers through the hair.

Silk excites romantic encounters and fantasies,
Bras and panties on a sultry afternoon,
The feel of flesh longing to be explored,
Kissed by lips trembling with anticipation,
An assortment of floral crops and yoga leggings
Held tenderly in an un-ironed moment,
Once selected for the wardrobe ensemble,
Replacing worn out personal memories
And excited now to be alive and on display.

Someday the laundry will be folded for the last time,
The cotton put in a box quietly at rest,
A chemise no longer enrapt in dance,
A camisole as formless as a whisper,
But for now my hands flatten out the wrinkles,
Try to smooth out every encounter,
Knowing that there is no way to do this right,
No way to lead this day into the night,
Without the eternal shadow of an inevitable hour.

Posthumously Yours

I thought that you would die first
So don't be too surprised
When you read this
Wondering how to balance
The checkbook and the other emotions

There's enough food in the freezer
For at least three weeks
The car is all paid off
As is the mortgage
Just hire an accountant
And talk with our attorney
Whoever that is

You won't need to make my side of the bed anymore
Worry about your prince being too cold
Needing extra blankets
Leaving fingerprints on the stainless-steel refrigerator
Just do my laundry once
And give it all to Goodwill

I'm trying not to write the line that makes you tear up
But you know that I could not live without you
So you will have to live without me
You can do it because I'll still be there
You'll see the signs
Like cookie crumbs on wooden floors
And photos that will make you laugh once more

We had a life that we knew from the start
Would last until death did us part
I'm sorry that I was the one to leave you hanging
I didn't mean to end the singing and dancing
With no more escargot
Or our view of Le Trocadéro
And turn the ending into a new beginning

A Dance Horizontal

Eyes that looked into each other's eyes

Somehow knew that everything had changed

Voices that talked gently back and forth

Rearranged the universe in moment after moment

Unlike every other day

In a way that was honest

Trusting in what we say

And meaning that we will stay

In love that finds itself

In different places and different times

Moving with emotion not choreographed

In its own rhythm and song

Companions growing old together

And trying to understand

Each burst of laughter or solemn moment

That move in bonded unison

Like wavelengths of harmony

Softly stroking the body and mind

With a caress deep into the soul

And mindful of motion and meaning

We can see beyond the horizon

Feel what only we can feel

And say everything that we can say

As we look into each other's eyes and dance

About the Author

Born in Manhattan, New York City, in 1947, Kenneth Lyon was raised on the Upper West Side and graduated from Clarkson College of Technology with a B.S. in Mathematics, The Johns Hopkins University Writing Seminars with an M.A. in Creative Writing Poetry, and the University of Denver with a Ph.D. in Creative Writing Fiction. Dr. Lyon was an educator for forty-five years, teaching at all levels in Maryland, Vermont, Colorado, China, and Washington State. He was also a school principal, a central administration director, and a Harassment, Intimidation, and Bullying Compliance Officer. After he retired, Dr. Lyon continued his anti-bullying work as a ventriloquist for five years, presenting with the figure Byron Stander at schools, clubs, various organizations, and the International Ventriloquist Society. Ken lives with his wife and dog in Palm Desert, California, and is an active member of Desert Poets.

Ken welcomes your comments at kenlyon@adancehorizontal.com.

Acknowledgements

A Dance Horizontal took a long time in coming, more than fifty years. The last four were filled with many days of intentional writing, yet I often woke up often in the middle of the night to compose half-asleep at my computer. All along the way, I have been whole-heartedly encouraged and supported by teachers, friends, and family.

Wes Craven (yes, *Nightmare on Elm Street* Wes Craven) was my sophomore Humanities teacher at Clarkson and the cameraman on *Pandora Experimentia*, a film that I co-authored and directed in 1968. After hearing me read poems at *The Pendulum* coffee house in Potsdam, he told me to apply to The Johns Hopkins University Writing Seminars, which he had attended. He wrote to the director, Elliott Coleman, and that summer I met with Coleman and read to him. He accepted me into the program on the spot and heavily influenced my writing for the following year, always appreciating my creativity and allowing me to experiment freely.

Colleagues from Hopkins and the University of Denver continue to share their writing with me, engage in literary conversations, and offer inspiration, much to my appreciation. Monthly meetings with Desert Poets provide a community for writing new verses and receiving critiques. I would like to thank Marilyn Gruen, Rick Kenny, Marvin Klapman, Natalie Kuyper, Rich Levenfeld, Florence Cassen Mayers, Cheryl Miller, Jean Sanchez, and Sharon Wolfe for reading my work and sharing their poetry with me.

Working with Robert McDowell was a major turning point. As a developmental editor, he read through all of the poems that I was trying to put into a publishable collection, commenting on those that he liked as well as some that either needed to go back to the drawing board or to the recycle bin. He picked at my rhymes and introduced me to the word "doggerel." I am deeply indebted to his expertise as a critic, his gentle, positive attitude, as well as his experience as a publisher. I would also like to thank Ray Rhamey, who designed this book. With a brilliant eye for layout, he worked relentlessly with me through numerous revisions in order to bring my poems to life on the printed page.

My sons have cheered me on, Aaron with his enthusiasm for my writing and accomplishments, and Sean for his willingness to read my poems and provide solid feedback. Above all, Roberta gave me the freedom to write and pursue my dreams. She constantly inspires me and lives one way or another in every poem. She has read them over and over again, editing and proofing, always commenting, nodding, or laughing. My dream became her dream, and she became my muse and my life.

A Dance Horizontal wouldn't be dancing without all of these people and many others.

Printed in the USA
CPSIA information can be obtained
at www.ICGtesting.com
LVHW050924181223
766490LV00067B/2004